Seasoned In Texas

The Adolphus Cookbook

Design and graphics by Oldfield Davis, Inc.

Photography by Robert Latorre

Typography by RR Publication & Production Co., Inc.

Coordinator — W. Jay Love

Printed by Taylor Publishing Company, Dallas, Texas

ISBN 0–9634101–0–5

Dedicated to our guests in Texas
and throughout the world
who have added the true flavor
to our seasons in Texas

Foreword

Writing *Seasoned in Texas: The Adolphus Cookbook* has been a desire since I started at The Adolphus in 1988. It seemed to be part of a natural progression that began with my training at the Culinary Institute of America and that has culminated in the extraordinarily rich experience at The Adolphus. With its impeccable reputation and its unqualified commitment to fine food, The Adolphus has offered me, as an executive chef, both challenging work and unrestrained creativity. Of such things good recipes are made — and from which great cookbooks evolve.

With this freedom has come the opportunity to create both a culinary identity for the hotel's three restaurants and memorable meals for such dignitaries as Queen Elizabeth and Prince Philip, First Lady Barbara Bush, and comedian Bill Cosby. In turn, this flexibility and exciting range has produced a file of recipes and anecdotes that together give a fascinating glimpse into our recent culinary history.

Naming the book *Seasoned in Texas* and organizing the recipes around the seasons came naturally. Professional chefs are very much influenced by the time of year when planning menus and selecting fresh ingredients. This is especially true at The Adolphus, where we take great pride in tailoring our cuisine to the special occasions that fill every calendar. There's a certain expectation among our guests, too, that when they check in for the night or tuck themselves in here for the weekend, we will offer them something far beyond the standard fare. From the velvety lobster bisque in The French Room to the fiery black bean chili in the Walt Garrison Rodeo Bar, The Adolphus' culinary tradition ensures that we never disappoint.

It's this tradition — blending rich classical training with modern, seasonal influences — that makes The Adolphus timeless in its execution. And the secret of our consistency, season after season, is the commitment to that ideal on the part of those who work in our kitchens every day.

Kevin Garvin
Executive Chef
The Adolphus

Foreword

With the opening of The Adolphus in 1912, Dallas became a member of an exclusive club of cities that offered travelers world class ambiance and cuisine. The hotel, from the very first, boasted European chefs and glorious food presentations unmatched in elegance and style. Nearly a century has past now, but that culinary distinction has neither dimmed in its brilliance nor been surpassed by its competitors. Like its European counterparts, The Adolphus has become consistently first rate in its cuisine, its service and its accommodations.

In 1981, The Adolphus saw a multi-million dollar restoration that added more splendor and sparkle to its sterling reputation. Since that time The Adolphus has been recognized internationally as one of less than 50 hotels to receive the coveted American Automobile Association Five Diamond Award. That award, which has been given to the hotel annually without fail, hangs proudly in our registration lobby to this day.

As a Texas landmark, the hotel is a reflection of the Lone Star State's grand traditions and wide-open friendliness. Its setting is magnificent but unpretentious; its staff, warm but not invasive. This unique blend of old world charm and Southern hospitality is exemplified in the work of Executive Chef Kevin Garvin.

An American trained by the European masters and steeped in our Texas heritage, Chef Garvin has taken The Adolphus kitchens to a new level of culinary excellence. His recipes — and, indeed, this book — celebrates the best of The Adolphus, and we are very proud of his accomplishments. Truly it can be said that this cookbook and The Adolphus are seasoned in Texas.

All of us at The Adolphus hope *Seasoned in Texas: The Adolphus Cookbook* recalls many happy meals and memories, for you and your family.

Garvin O'Neil
Managing Director
The Adolphus

SEASONED IN TEXAS

Table of Contents

Spring

Summer

Autumn

Winter

Acknowledgments

The ingredients for a great cookbook are very much like the ingredients for a great recipe. Only the best will do.

Seasoned in Texas would not have been possible without the kind and generous contribution of time, talent, and merchandise of Neiman Marcus Downtown. The Public Relations, Visual, and Gift Galleries departments at this extraordinary store spent many hours helping to create the perfect setting for each photograph. Their enthusiasm and attention to detail were rare and precious ingredients and made all the difference.

This book would never have happened without the extra efforts of Brent, Chris, the two Mikes, Russell, Roberto and Bruce. They, along with the rest of the hotel's culinary team, are the secret ingredients in preparing our guests' favorite dishes throughout the year.

Jean Banchet, whose inspiration and years of experience have kept The Adolphus in the forefront of fine dining, also deserves much applause and a very warm "Bravo!" from all of us.

Special thanks are also due Williams-Sonoma, Don Snell Buick/Range Rover, Bonnie and Ted Swinney of Anteks, and the Cotton Bowl. Their staffs were accommodating and gracious no matter how tall the order. Essential ingredients, to be sure.

The superb work of Rachel Davis, Kerry Schroeder, Janice Metcalfe, Stephanie Armstrong, Steve Majors, and floral artist Luther Menke was invaluable in completing every chapter. Their enthusiasm and eye for detail significantly enhanced the other ingredients.

To Anne Hanrahan, whose wizardry on the computer and patience in collating paper after paper, not to mention handling her other responsibilities, a warm thank you.

Without the ability of David Davis to put all the thoughts, ideas and recipes into a clear and concise book form, this project may have never gotten off the ground. Great job, David!

Throughout the planning and preparation of this book Betsy Field wore many hats: editor, stylist, assistant photographer, sous chef, chauffeur, and visionary. This book benefited greatly from her insights, creativity, and wise counsel.

To the many others who added the final touches and the garnishments, a heartfelt thank you. You brought out the flavor — in a dash and a pinch — and made the book the best it could be.

SPRING

AT THE ADOLPHUS

SPRING

In 1991 The Adolphus was selected by
Buckingham Palace to host Her Majesty
Queen Elizabeth II and His Royal
Highness Prince Philip, the Duke of
Edinburgh. Months of planning went
into the preparations for The Queen's
visit. From sending sample menus to
Buckingham Palace and rehearsing
"God Save the Queen" to coaching the staff
on royal protocol and etiquette,
no detail was overlooked in making
Her Majesty's stay flawless. The security
was impeccable, with both Scotland Yard
and the U.S. Secret Service accepting the
responsibility — down to sending guard
dogs to "inspect" the kitchens and
conducting background checks on all
hotel staff who would be preparing and
serving The Queen's meals.

SPRING

A ROYAL VISIT

Clear Chicken Broth with Spring Vegetables
and Herb Dumplings

Stuffed Breast of Chicken filled with
Seasonal Mushrooms

Summer Pudding filled with Seasonal Berries
on a Vanilla Cream Painting

❖

(selected items pictured on page 33)

Makes 4 one-cup portions.

Clear Chicken Broth

1   *natural chicken, cut into*
     8 pieces

1   *medium size carrot*

1   *medium size onion*

2   *ribs celery*

3   *sprigs parsley*

3   *sprigs fresh thyme*

2   *cloves garlic*

8   *black peppercorns*

Rinse the chicken with water. Put the chicken in a large pot and cover with cold water. Place over high heat and bring to a boil. Remove the pot from the stove, drain the chicken and rinse well with cold water. Add the rest of the ingredients and pour in enough cold water to cover the chicken. Bring the water back to a boil and reduce to a simmer. Cook the broth for 2 hours. Occasionally skim the broth to remove the scum and fat. When the broth is ready, strain it through a sieve.

From the chef:

For a richer flavor, reduce the broth by one-half. This simple and basic broth can be frozen, too. Try freezing it in ice cube trays; the cubes make it very convenient.

Herb Dumplings

4 eggs
2½ cups flour
½ cup milk
¼ stick butter, melted
2 teaspoons baking powder
Fresh herbs
Salt and pepper to taste

Combine eggs, milk, and butter in a mixing bowl. Add dry ingredients and mix with a spoon to form a damp dough. (You may want to use your hands to help work the dough and eliminate any lumps.)

Bring a pot of salted water to a boil. After forming dumplings by hand, carefully drop the dumplings into the water and simmer until the dumplings nearly double in size. This will take approximately 10 minutes. Remove dumplings from the water with a slotted spoon and serve.

From the chef:

The number of dumplings this recipe makes depends on how large you make the dumplings.

Spring Vegetables

1 carrot
1 zucchini
1 summer squash
½ cup snow peas

Cut each vegetable into small pieces suitable for a soup garnish. If desired, blanch vegetables by bringing them to a boil for 50 seconds and then shocking them in an ice-water bath. Add the vegetables to the soup right before serving.

Makes 6 servings.

Luncheon Entree prepared by Chef Kevin Garvin
for
Queen Elizabeth II and Prince Philip, Duke of Edinburgh

Stuffed Breast of Chicken

6 *chicken breasts, boneless and skinless*

1 *large head Nappa cabbage*

½ *cup white table wine*

½ *cup shiitake mushrooms*

¼ *cup chanterelle mushrooms*

2 *cups white mushrooms*

1 *whole shallot*

2 *cloves garlic (optional...not for Her Majesty)*

¼ *white onion*

2 *tablespoons olive oil*

2 *sprigs clean thyme*

Salt and pepper to taste

Cover a clean work surface with plastic wrap and lay chicken breasts on top. Cover the breasts with another sheet of plastic wrap. Flatten the breasts by pounding them very lightly with a meat mallet. Wrap the breasts in a new sheet of plastic wrap and refrigerate.

Bring a large pot of water to a boil. While waiting for the water to boil, remove the leaves from the core of the cabbage and rinse well. Plunge the leaves — a few at a time — into the boiling water for 30 seconds. Remove with a pair of tongs and chill quickly in an ice-water bath. Quickly remove the leaves from the ice bath and pat dry between two paper towels. Keep the leaves between the towels until ready to use.

In a food processor fitted with a metal blade, place the shallots, garlic, onion and all of the mushrooms. (If Queen Elizabeth II is on the guest list, do not use garlic.) Blend the ingredients until they are very fine. Transfer the blended mushrooms to a heavy-bottomed

(continued)

Stuffed Breast of Chicken continued

saucepan that contains the heated olive oil. Sauté for 2 minutes. Pour in the white wine and continue cooking until the liquid has almost evaporated. Add thyme, salt and pepper to taste. Cool completely.

Lay out a new piece of plastic wrap (approximately 12" × 12") on a clean work surface. Place 4 cabbage leaves in the middle of the plastic wrap and arrange them so they overlap one another by about 2 inches. Put the chicken breast on top and season lightly with salt and pepper. Spoon some of the blended mushrooms on top of the chicken breast and spread evenly. Roll up the chicken breast, leaving the mushroom mixture inside. Then wrap the cabbage leaves completely around the chicken breast.

Tie each chicken breast with butcher string and bake in a preheated 350°F oven for 14 to 18 minutes. Remove from the oven and let rest for 10 minutes before slicing.

From the chef:

The selection of mushrooms can vary. Another type of cabbage that can be used is savoy; regular green cabbage can be used, but only the larger leaves.

Makes 6 servings.

Summer Pudding with Seasonal Berries

8-10 *slices white sandwich bread*

2 *cups simple syrup*

2 *pints raspberries*

2 *pints strawberries*

2 *pints blueberries*

1 *tablespoon lemon juice*

1 *cinnamon stick*

¼ *cup cassis liqueur (optional)*

2 *tablespoons gelatin*

½ *cup cold water*

Using a round pastry cutter, cut bread to line the bottom and sides of 6 tea or soup cups which have been lightly oiled with salad oil.

Bring the simple syrup, 1 pint of each of the berries, lemon juice, cinnamon stick and liqueur to a boil in a medium saucepan. Boil for 5 minutes, remove from heat and strain.

Let gelatin stand for 5 to 10 minutes in the cold water before adding it to the warm berry juice.

Fill lined cups with the remaining berries. (You may not need all of the berries.) Pour juice mixture over the berries, allowing the juice to soak into the fruit and bread slices. Cover the tops of the puddings with plates that fit snugly. Weigh down the plates to compress the puddings. Refrigerate overnight.

To serve, remove the puddings from the cups by sticking the cups in a shallow pan of hot water for a minute or two. The puddings should drop out easily when inverted. Place the puddings on plates and drizzle with vanilla cream (recipe on following page).

From the chef:

This is a great dessert for a summer barbecue. Other varieties of berries may be substituted depending on what is in season. It can be served alone or with whipped cream or ice cream. Try rubbing the inside of the cups with brown sugar before lining with bread.

Vanilla Cream

See pastry cream on page 32. Thin the pastry cream with a small amount of heavy cream and, if desired, a liqueur such as Kirsch or Grand Marnier.

SPRING

The *New York Times* has called
The French Room "a Louis XV fantasy on
the prairie," and this is particularly true at
Easter. Mothers and daughters in
matching dresses and bonnets, fathers and
sons in their Sunday best bring a parade
of high fashion that rivals Ascot on
opening day. Reservations for this elegant
brunch are sought after, and many
families have standing reservations,
having made it a part of their Eastertide
traditions. Each year the chefs spend
months testing recipes, selecting the finest
cuts of meats, and hand-picking the fruits
and vegetables. They work hard to
achieve a delicate balance between old
favorites and new trends.

EASTER BRUNCH

Lobster Salad with Sweet Mangoes

Avocado Gazpacho with Tomatillos

Softly Scrambled Eggs with Fresh Herbs on
Skillet-fried Canadian Bacon and
Crisp Brioche Croutons

Jalapeño Cheese Grits with Sweet Apricots

Feuilletée of Raspberries with Caramel Sauce

❖

Brunch after church on Easter Sunday

(selected items pictured on page 34)

Lobster Salad with Sweet Mangoes

4 lobsters, 1 pound each

2 ounces field greens, cleaned

Mint vinaigrette
(recipe on following page)

2 fresh mangoes, peeled and diced

1 cup mango purée

1 cup white wine

2 cups chicken stock (optional)

3 cloves garlic, peeled and crushed

2 shallots, peeled and chopped

1 serrano chile pepper, seeded

1 teaspoon chopped cilantro

1 teaspoon chopped basil

1 tablespoon olive oil

1 tomato, peeled, seeded and diced

In a pot of salted boiling water, place live lobsters and cook for 6 to 7 minutes. Then shock them in ice water. Remove meat from shells and dice into one-inch pieces. Reserve meat and shells.

Heat olive oil in a heavy saucepan over medium heat. Add lobster shells, garlic, shallots, and serrano pepper. Sweat without coloration, then pour in white wine and reduce until almost dry. Add chicken stock, mango purée, cilantro and basil. Bring to a boil and simmer for 30 minutes. Strain with a colander and discard shells.

Put strained liquid into a saucepan and return to heat. Add diced mangoes and cook until mango dice are soft. Then blend and strain the sauce. Refrigerate.

Pour mango sauce on each dinner plate. Toss field greens and lobster with vinaigrette and arrange in the center of the plate. Garnish with diced tomatoes.

From the chef:

This is a large salad and may be served as a main course.

Mint Vinaigrette

1 cup fresh mint leaves and
stems

½ cup parsley stems

1 cup olive oil

⅓ cup vinegar

1 clove garlic, finely diced

1 shallot bulb, finely diced

½ cup strong flavored chicken
broth

Salt and pepper to taste

In a blender or food processor, combine the vinegar, garlic and diced shallot. Blend well for 6 seconds. Add chicken broth, mint and parsley. Blend on minimum speed. Slowly add the olive oil until the vinaigrette starts to thicken. Check the seasoning: you may want to add more vinegar or more mint leaves for flavor and color. Finish the vinaigrette with salt and pepper to taste.

From the chef:

Use a small blender for best results. When using a food processor, blend the vinaigrette longer.

Avocado Gazpacho with Tomatillos

6   ripe avocados, peeled, seeded
    and diced (small dice)

10 roasted tomatillos, husks
    removed and diced (small
    dice)

1   cucumber, peeled, seeded and
    diced (small dice)

1   green pepper, seeded and
    diced (small dice)

1   red pepper, seeded and diced
    (small dice)

2   stalks celery, diced (small
    dice)

2   green onions, diced (small
    dice)

    Lime juice to taste

    Lemon juice to taste

1   onion, diced (small dice)

1   teaspoon chili powder

1   teaspoon cayenne pepper

1   cup V-8 Juice

2   tablespoons olive oil

    Salt and white pepper

1   can (10½ ounces) chicken
    broth

After dicing all of the vegetables, put them in a mixing bowl with the rest of the ingredients. Regulate the consistency of the gazpacho by adjusting the amount of the liquids added; this, of course, depends on personal taste.

From the chef:

To ensure that the gazpacho is well chilled and that all of the flavors have time to marry, make the gazpacho 2 to 3 hours before serving. We sometimes put the gazpacho in the freezer to ensure that it is very cold.

Softly Scrambled Eggs on Canadian Bacon

12 large eggs, whisked together

½ cup fresh herbs (e.g., thyme, chervil, basil), chopped

¼ cup sour cream

8 slices Canadian bacon

¼ pound butter (for sautéing)

1 loaf brioche, cut into ½-inch slices (recipe page 35)

Jalapeño cheese grits with sweet apricots

Optional:

Asparagus or broccoli, freshly steamed

Fresh seasonal fruit, diced

From the chef:

If desired, freshly steamed asparagus or broccoli and fresh fruit can be served in place of the jalapeño cheese grits.

Combine eggs, fresh herbs, and sour cream in a stainless steel mixing bowl. Set mixture aside.

Using a round cookie cutter, cut brioche slices into eight 2½-inch rounds. Melt a small amount of butter in a Teflon pan and brown the brioche rounds on both sides. (To ensure even browning, do this slowly using low to medium heat.) Remove rounds from the pan and keep warm. Do not cover or the croutons will become soft.

In the same pan, heat a small amount of butter and sauté the Canadian bacon on both sides (approximately 30 seconds on each side). Remove the slices from the pan, cover, and keep warm.

Wipe the Teflon pan with a soft cloth and return it to the stove. Using a low to medium flame, heat some of the butter slowly and add the egg mixture. Stir the eggs constantly with a wooden spoon or flat wooden spatula and cook slowly until the eggs have become soft scrambled.

Place the brioche croutons on individual serving plates and lay the Canadian bacon slices on the croutons. Spoon even amounts of the scrambled eggs on top of the Canadian bacon. Finish the plates with sprigs of fresh herbs. Serve the jalapeño cheese grits with sweet apricots (recipe on following page) on warm side plates.

Jalapeño Cheese Grits with Sweet Apricots

4	*cups milk*
2	*cups water*
1½	*cups quick grits*
2	*cups grated cheddar cheese*
2	*large eggs, beaten*
8	*tablespoons butter*
½	*teaspoon salt*
2	*cloves garlic, minced*
10	*fresh jalapeños, roasted, peeled, seeded and diced (small dice)*
15	*fresh apricots, halved and pitted*
¼	*cup brown sugar*

Heat oven to 350°F.

In a one-quart sauce pot, combine the milk, water, 4 tablespoons of butter and salt. Bring to a boil and stir in the grits. Reduce to a simmer until the grits thicken, stirring frequently for about 2 to 3 minutes. Slowly add some of the grits to the eggs to temper them. Pour egg mixture back into the pan with the remaining grits and add cheese and diced roasted jalapeños. Put grits mixture back on stove on low heat until cheese is melted. Rub a 6" × 8" baking pan with 1 tablespoon of butter and the minced garlic. Pour grits mixture into the pan and arrange the apricot halves on top of the grits. Sprinkle the apricots with brown sugar and dot each apricot with butter. Bake the grits for 30 to 40 minutes until tops are a light golden brown and slightly puffy. Remove from the oven and spoon portions onto warm plates.

Roasted Jalapeños:

Heat oven to 350°F.

Rub jalapeños with vegetable oil and place on a sheet pan. Place in the oven for 5 to 10 minutes or until skin becomes a little wrinkled. Remove from oven and cool. Using a paring knife, remove the stem, skin and seeds, and discard. Be sure to wash hands thoroughly after handling the peppers.

Feuilletée of Raspberries

2 sheets puff pastry dough

2 cups pastry cream
 (recipe on following page)

½ cup heavy cream

2 tablespoons sugar

½ pints fresh raspberries

While puff pastry is cold, cut out six 2½" × 4" rectangles. Place rectangles on papered cookie sheet and bake in a 400°F oven for about 15 minutes.

In a small mixing bowl, whip heavy cream with sugar until soft peaks form. Set aside. In another small bowl, whip cooled pastry cream until smooth. Carefully fold the whipped cream into the pastry cream until incorporated.

When puff pastry has cooled, slice in half lengthwise. Spread a generous amount of pastry cream over bottom half of each rectangle and top with fresh raspberries. Place top half of rectangle over raspberries and dust with powdered sugar. Serve with caramel sauce.

From the chef:

Feuilletés should be assembled and served immediately so the texture stays crisp. Also, try using other fruits and berries. All will work nicely with this recipe.

Pastry Cream

2 cups milk

4 egg yolks

¼ cup granulated sugar

3 tablespoons corn starch

2 tablespoons cake flour

1 teaspoon vanilla

Bring milk to a boil and remove from heat. In a bowl, mix egg yolks with sugar until smooth. Stir in cornstarch and flour. Pour half of the hot milk into the egg mixture, then return all of it to the remaining hot milk. Stir over low heat until it boils and thickens. Add vanilla and cool.

Caramel Sauce

⅓ cup water

10 tablespoons sugar

2 cups heavy cream

2 tablespoons butter

Pour water into medium saucepan and add the sugar. Cook over medium heat until mixture begins to boil. Wash down the inside of the pan with a pastry brush dipped in cold water so that no crystals form. Continue cooking until sugar turns a deep amber color and the surface begins to smoke slightly. Remove from heat and immediately add butter and cream. Stir constantly with a whisk until well incorporated. Cool.

From the chef:

This recipe has been a mainstay in The French Room for years. The demand has become so great that we now do variations in our banquet department and The Bistro.

A Royal Visit, p. 17
and *Easter Brunch*, p. 25

Her Majesty
Queen Elizabeth II

Brioche

4 cups plus 2 tablespoons
bread flour

3 tablespoons sugar

1½ teaspoons salt

⅓ cup milk

2½ tablespoons instant yeast

3 tablespoons melted butter

½ cup softened butter

Heat oven to 350°F.

In a mixing bowl, combine flour, sugar, salt, milk, eggs, yeast and melted butter. Mix ingredients together with a dough hook for approximately two minutes. Let the dough rest in the bowl for 30 to 45 minutes. Add the remaining butter and mix until the butter is completely incorporated. Let the dough rest for another ½ hour. Meanwhile, prepare 2 loaf pans with a spray release. Divide the dough into equal balls. Place the dough in the prepared loaf pans and cover with a moist towel. Then put the pans in a warm area and let the dough rise for 1 to 2 hours. Bake the bread for 20 to 30 minutes. Remove from the oven and cool on a rack.

From the chef:

Brioche can be used just like any other bread because of its high quantity of butter and sugar. It is excellent with French food.

SPRING

Spring brings a softness to Dallas that can be seen in the wild flowers that dust the parks and boulevards, and that can be felt in the light, cool breezes that circulate the season's delicate aromas. Everyone seems drawn to brunch on carefree Saturday mornings or after church on Sundays. On these days The Bistro is a blur of activity. Waiters follow a fast-paced choreography. Smiles and deep Southern drawls can be found at every table. It's a snapshot of spring in Texas.

BISTRO BRUNCH

Fresh Fruit Smoothies

Toasted Granola with Raisins, Nuts
and Shredded Coconut

Maple-Pecan French Toast

Chocolate Croissants

Memom's Coffee Cake

❖

(selected items pictured on page 51)

Fresh Fruit Smoothies

Strawberry-banana

3	strawberries
¼	banana
½	cup low-fat plain yogurt
½	cup skim milk
½	teaspoon brown sugar

Place fruit in a blender and purée. Add milk, yogurt and sugar. Blend until smooth and well incorporated. Pour into a glass and serve chilled.

Makes 2 one-half cup servings.

Chocolate-banana

½	banana
½	cup yogurt
½	cup skim milk
2	tablespoons chocolate syrup

Place fruit in a blender and purée. Add milk, yogurt and chocolate syrup. Blend until smooth and well incorporated. Pour into a glass and serve chilled.

Makes 2 one-half cup servings.

(continued)

Fresh Fruit Smoothies continued

Strawberry

6 strawberries
½ cup yogurt
½ cup skim milk
½ teaspoon brown sugar

Place fruit in a blender and purée. Add milk, yogurt and sugar. Blend until smooth and well incorporated. Pour into a glass and serve chilled.

Makes 2 one-half cup servings.

Pineapple-papaya

⅛ pineapple, diced
¼ papaya
½ cup yogurt
½ cup skim milk
½ teaspoon brown sugar

Place fruit in a blender and purée. Add milk, yogurt and sugar. Blend until smooth and well incorporated. Pour into a glass and serve chilled.

Makes 2 one-half cup servings.

From the chef:

Smoothies are best when served fresh. If you have any left over, refrigerate and blend briefly before serving.

Makes 8 to 12 servings.

Toasted Granola

4   cups quick oats

¾   cup honey

½   cup packed brown sugar

¼   pound butter

1   tablespoon cinnamon

1   tablespoon vanilla

¼   cup almond slices

¼   cup pecan pieces

¼   cup coconut flakes

¼   cup raisins

Place the butter, honey, brown sugar, cinnamon and vanilla in a medium saucepan. Melt the mixture over medium heat, stirring occasionally. Once the mixture is melted remove from heat and add the oatmeal, almonds, pecans, and coconut. Mix until well incorporated.

Place the granola mixture on a cookie sheet and bake for approximately 15 minutes in a 325°F oven. Mixture should be golden brown. Stir frequently so the mixture will brown evenly without burning. Remove the granola from the oven and cool. Add the raisins and store in an airtight container when cool.

From the chef:

When the granola has cooled enough to touch, break up the pieces with your hands. Don't eat too much too soon!

Maple-Pecan French Toast

8 slices cinnamon-raisin
   Texas-sliced bread

6 eggs, well beaten

½ cup heavy cream

1½ teaspoon vanilla

1 teaspoon cinnamon

¼ teaspoon nutmeg

3 cups pecans, finely chopped

½ pound butter

1 cup maple syrup

Place eggs in a mixing bowl. Whisk in the heavy cream, vanilla, cinnamon and nutmeg. Soak the bread in the egg mixture for 5 to 10 seconds and then coat with the pecans.

In a large skillet, heat the butter over medium heat and sauté the bread on each side until the pecans are golden brown (approximately three minutes, depending on how hot the skillet is). Transfer the French toast to a cookie sheet and place in a 350°F oven. Bake for 5 to 10 minutes. Remove toast from the oven and slice diagonally. Serve immediately with warm maple syrup.

From the chef:

Any kind of bread may be used. However, the baking times will vary. Sprinkle with powdered sugar before serving. (Texas-sliced bread is thickly sliced bread, for those not from the Lone Star State.)

Makes approximately 1 dozen.

Chocolate Croissants

2½ cups high gluten flour

2 tablespoons granulated sugar

1 ounce butter, softened

⅛ cup instant yeast

¾ cup cold milk

1½ sticks soft butter

2 eggs mixed with one tablespoon water for wash

18 ounces semisweet chocolate (chopped)

Mix dry ingredients with butter and yeast. Pour in cold milk and mix with a dough hook at medium speed for 5 minutes. Dough should be smooth and elastic. Form into a ball and cover with plastic wrap. Let rise in a warm place until it doubles in size.

On a floured surface, roll out dough to form a rectangle. Place softened butter in center. Fold both ends, then turn and fold over open ends to make another rectangle. Chill for 1 hour in the refrigerator.

Roll dough out lengthwise. Fold both ends toward center, then one half over the other. Roll out lengthwise again and fold one end to the middle and cover with the other end. Sprinkle with flour. Wrap in plastic wrap and refrigerate overnight.

Roll dough out lengthwise again, using a little flour for easier handling. Fold ends one over the other at the center. Turn dough over and adjust its position so the folded edges are crosswise in front of you. Roll it out again away from you to form a rectangle approximately 6" × 18".

Chocolate Croissants continued

Begin forming triangles by cutting a strip from a corner to four inches from the opposite corner. Then cut across to make a triangle with a 4-inch edge on the first side. Continue until all of the dough is cut into triangles.

Take one triangle at a time and stretch it slightly, starting at the wide end. Place approximately 1½ ounces of chopped chocolate in the center of each triangle (near the wide end). Roll it toward you, pressing slightly, with the two ends brought to a curve to make the crescent shape.

Place each on a baking sheet lined with paper. Brush with egg wash mixture and allow to rise in a warm place for approximately 1½ hours or until they double in size. Bake at 400°F for 15 to 20 minutes.

From the chef:

This recipe requires a lot of work; it's probably not a recipe for the novice baker.

Makes 9 to 12 servings.

Memom's Coffee Cake

3 cups flour

2 cups sugar

  Pinch salt

2½ teaspoons baking powder

½ pound butter, softened

1 teaspoon vanilla

1 cup milk

3 eggs

1¼ teaspoons cinnamon

Preheat oven to 350°F.

Combine flour, sugar, salt and baking powder. Cut in the butter until mixture is crumbly. Reserve 1 cup of crumb mixture for topping. Add vanilla, milk and eggs and beat until smooth. Grease and flour a 13" × 9" cake pan and pour the batter into the pan. Sprinkle the reserved crumb mixture over the batter. Then sprinkle with cinnamon and bake for 45 minutes. Cool in the pan and cut into squares.

From the chef:

This is another recipe that is often requested. Enjoy!

SPRING

Room service at a grand hotel is a luxury for the guest and always a challenge for the kitchen. Getting gourmet food to its destination hot and on time is a daily test that often separates good hotels from great ones. On a typical morning at The Adolphus, room service is the busiest kitchen in the hotel. For honeymoon couples and weekenders, breakfast in bed is a way of adding to the romance of relaxed, sleepy mornings. They can snuggle up in their plush Adolphus robes and let breakfast come to them. Our celebrity guests greatly appreciate the privacy room service affords. They can eat uninterrupted in their suites, far from the public eye. Behind the scenes, the rich and famous bring a special excitement to guest-room dining. Bill Cosby, one of our favorites, calls in his own orders and delights the kitchen staff with his jokes and cooking instructions.

BREAKFAST IN BED

Warm Belgian Waffles with
Maple Syrup and Whipped Cream

Candied Peaches in Syrup

Blueberry Muffins

Sun-dried Cherry Jam

❖

(selected items pictured on page 52)

Makes four 6" waffles.

Belgian Waffles

½ cup milk

2 tablespoons butter, melted

1 egg cup

1 cup flour

2 teaspoons baking powder

3 tablespoons sugar

½ teaspoon salt

Combine the milk, butter and egg and beat lightly. Combine the flour, baking powder, sugar, and salt and add to the milk mixture. Cook in a Belgian waffle maker following manufacturer's directions.

From the chef:

If you are fortunate enough to have real maple syrup, heat it before serving. It can be heated in either a water bath or a microwave oven.

Making whipped cream can be very frustrating. It takes too long by hand and a mixer can be more trouble than it's worth. To overcome some of the frustration, leave a small stainless steel mixing bowl and flexible whip in the freezer overnight. The whipping will go quicker when the utensils are ice cold.

Candied Peaches in Syrup

10 fresh peaches

4 ounces butter

1½ cups sugar (variable)

Lemon juice to taste

4 ounces raspberry liqueur or
brandy

Scald the peaches in a large pot of boiling water for 1 to 2 minutes to loosen the skins. Remove and shock in ice water to stop the cooking process. Peel and slice the peaches. The size and shape of the slices can vary.

In a large saucepan, melt the butter. Add the peaches, sugar and liqueur. Cook over moderate heat, stirring occasionally until the peaches are soft but not mushy. Finish to the desired tartness with lemon juice.

From the chef:

The compote may take less sugar than the recipe calls for. It should not be too sweet.

Makes 2 dozen.

Blueberry Muffins

1   cup soft butter
1½ cups sugar
1   teaspoon salt
3   large eggs
6   cups sifted flour
1½ tablespoons baking powder
3   cups milk
2   pints blueberries

Place butter, sugar, and salt in a large mixing bowl and cream until light and fluffy. Scrape sides of bowl and add eggs, one at a time. Mixture should be well blended. Add flour and baking powder. Continue to mix until thoroughly blended. Slowly pour in milk to incorporate the batter. With a large wooden spoon or spatula, gently fold in blueberries. (Be careful not to mash the berries.)

Pour batter into greased muffin tins, filling each "cup" ⅔ full. Bake at 350°F for approximately 20 to 25 minutes.

From the chef:

Coat the blueberries with flour before blending, as this will keep the blueberries from falling to the bottom of the muffin tins.

Bistro Brunch, p. 37

Sun-dried Cherry Jam

2½ cups sugar

⅔ cup water

4 cups sun-dried cherries

½ cup water

Place sugar and ⅔ cup water in a medium saucepan and bring to a boil over high heat. Continue cooking until sugar reaches 140°C (284°F).

While sugar is cooking, soften cherries in a bowl of warm water. After a few minutes, strain cherries and roughly purée in a blender with ½ cup of water. Once sugar reaches correct temperature, add cherries. Continue cooking for approximately 10 minutes, or until mixture coats the back of a spoon. Cool.

From the chef:

If you would like to experiment making different kinds of jams, invest in a candy thermometer. It is money well spent.

Breakfast in Bed, p. 47

SUMMER

AT THE ADOLPHUS

SUMMER

Grilling. It's as American as apple pie — and the 4th of July. Most people do not associate The Adolphus with grilled foods. But our kitchens are equipped to handle everything from hamburgers to swordfish, and these and other tantalizing grilled meats are routinely listed on our menus. This is especially true during the steamy summer months in Dallas, when everyone wants a taste of outdoor cooking indoors. Independence Day in Big D can find the temperature skyrocketing to 100 degrees! Guests who spend that night in our Skylight Suites, though, can watch the fireworks in cool comfort as they enjoy a late night supper and toast the U.S.A.

GRILLING

Grilled Prawns on Rosemary Skewers

Grilled Lamb T-bones with a Port Wine
Barbecue Sauce

Grilled Chicken Breast with an
Ancho-Jalapeño Vinaigrette

Grilled Breast of Chicken in a
Jalapeño-Cilantro Marinade

Grilled Top-butt Sirloin Steaks Oriental-Style

Grilled Swordfish in a Tomato-Basil Marinade

Grilled Pork Tenderloin with a Coarse Ground
Mustard and Mint Marinade

Grilled Corn-on-the-Cob

Grilled New Potatoes

Roasted Sweet Peppers

❖

(selected items pictured on page 69)

Makes 4 servings.

Grilled Prawns on Rosemary Skewers

16 jumbo prawns
½ cup olive oil
¼ cup rosemary leaves
2 tablespoons garlic, crushed
2 tablespoons shallots, crushed
   Salt and pepper to taste
4 large rosemary stems,
   approximately 8 inches long

Remove the shell and leave only the tail on the prawns. With a paring knife, make a small incision down the back of the length of the prawn approximately ½-inch deep. Rinse the prawns under cold running water, removing any dirt.

Combine the rest of the ingredients in a mixing bowl (except for the rosemary stems). Place the prawns in this mixture and marinate for one hour.

Remove the rosemary leaves from each stem, except for 1½ inches. Skewer the prawns along the stem up to the remaining rosemary leaves. Grill over hot coals until prawns are no longer opaque and their flesh turns white.

From the chef:

Soak the rosemary skewers in water for at least 1 hour before grilling. Also make sure the prawns are skewered twice on the stem: once through the fat end and once through the end closest to the tail. This will prevent the prawns from falling through the grill grates.

Grilled Lamb T-bones
with a Port Wine Barbecue Sauce

6   lamb T-bones

2   cups ketchup

3   tablespoons tomato paste

¼   cup white vinegar

¼   cup steak sauce

3   tablespoons Worcestershire sauce

½   cup port wine (ruby)

2   tablespoons garlic, finely chopped

1   tablespoon shallots, finely chopped

1   tablespoon ginger, crushed

1   small onion, finely chopped

2   tablespoons brown sugar

1   tablespoon chili powder

1   teaspoon English mustard

1   teaspoon liquid smoke

¼   cup honey

Bring to a boil the port wine, garlic, ginger, shallots and onion. Reduce to ⅓. Add rest of ingredients and simmer for 2½ hours. The barbecue sauce can be strained, depending on individual taste. Its consistency, however, *should* be checked so that the sauce doesn't become too thick. Add water if it needs to be thinned.

Makes approximately 1 quart.

From the chef:

Have butcher cut lamb T-bones from the loin of the lamb. T-bones should be approximately ¾-inch thick; two chops are usually enough for one person. Marinate the lamb for approximately one hour before grilling. While grilling, remember to baste the chops with the port wine barbecue sauce.

Makes 6 servings.

Grilled Chicken Breast
with an Ancho-Jalapeño Vinaigrette

6   *chicken breasts*

4   *large ancho peppers, roasted and seeds removed*

2   *jalapeño peppers, roasted and seeds removed*

1½   *cups olive oil*

½   *cup red wine vinegar*

1   *bunch cilantro, diced*

2   *cloves garlic, diced*

1   *shallot bulb, diced*

½   *bunch parsley, chopped*

  Salt and pepper to taste

  Juice of two limes

Rub the jalapeño and ancho peppers with a little olive oil. Place in a 350°F oven and roast until pepper skins blister. Take from oven and remove the seeds. Put peppers and the remaining ingredients in a food processor. Slowly add the olive oil in a slow, steady stream.

Marinate the chicken breasts for ½ hour before grilling.

Makes 2½ cups of vinaigrette.

From the chef:

To remove the seeds from the ancho peppers, cut them down the side. Pull the peppers apart and remove the seeds. If you prefer, the skins can also be removed.

Grilled Breast of Chicken
in a Jalapeño-Cilantro Marinade

6 chicken breasts

2 jalapeño peppers, diced

½ cup olive oil

1 bunch cilantro

2 cloves garlic, crushed

   Juice of two limes

¼ cup chopped fresh herbs

1 teaspoon crushed cumin
   (optional)

1 teaspoon chili powder
   (optional)

   Salt and pepper to taste

Combine all of the ingredients. Let chicken breasts marinate for 1 hour. Before grilling, wipe the chicken breasts with a paper towel and remove most of the marinade.

From the chef:

Try seasoning the chicken with fresh herbs such as thyme, basil, rosemary and fennel. Mixing the herbs will give the grilled chicken breasts a robust flavor. Remember to baste the chicken breasts with the marinade while grilling.

Makes 6 servings.

Grilled Top-butt Sirloin Steaks Oriental-Style

6	*seven-ounce top-butt steaks*
1	*cup soy sauce*
2	*tablespoons sesame oil*
2	*tablespoons garlic, crushed*
1	*tablespoon shallots, crushed*
1	*bunch green onions, diced*
2	*tablespoons garlic chili paste*
1	*tablespoon fresh ginger, crushed*
½	*cup salad oil*

In a food processor fitted with a metal blade or in a stainless bowl using a wire whisk, combine the soy sauce, garlic, shallots, garlic chili paste and fresh ginger. Add the sesame oil and salad oil in a slow, steady stream while the food processor is running; or, if using a wire whisk, whisk vigorously to incorporate the oils. Add the diced green onions last. Marinate the steaks for one hour before grilling.

Makes approximately 2 cups of marinade.

From the chef:

The center-cut top-butt sirloin steak is ideal for grilling, but a beef tenderloin or strip-loin cut will also work well in this recipe.

Grilled Swordfish in a Tomato-Basil Marinade

6 *six-ounce swordfish steaks*

6 *very ripe Roma tomatoes*

3 *medium size very ripe beefsteak tomatoes*

¾ *cup fresh basil leaves, rough chopped*

1 *tablespoon garlic, crushed*

1 *tablespoon shallots, crushed*

½ *cup olive oil*

½ *cup salad oil*

½ *cup balsamic vinegar*

Salt and pepper to taste

In a food processor fitted with a metal blade, combine the tomatoes, garlic, shallots and balsamic vinegar. Blend for 5 to 10 seconds on high speed. Turn processor down to low and add the oils in a slow, steady stream. Finish with chopped basil leaves. Adjust seasoning with salt and pepper. Marinate the swordfish for one hour before grilling.

From the chef:

Be sure to remove most of the marinade before grilling. This will keep the swordfish steaks from becoming too brown.

Grilled Pork Tenderloin
with Mustard and Mint Marinade

2   *tablespoons white wine vinegar*

2   *tablespoons Pommery mustard*

Salt and coarse black pepper to taste

½   *cup salad oil*

¼   *cup fresh mint leaves, chopped*

2   *tablespoons shallots, coarsely chopped*

2   *tablespoons garlic, coarsely chopped*

6   *five-ounce portions pork tenderloin (1½ to 2 pounds)*

In a food processor fitted with a metal blade, blend the vinegar, mustard, salt, pepper, shallots and garlic for 10 seconds. Turn the processor off and scrape the sides of the bowl. Turn the machine back on and pour in the oil in a slow, steady stream. Remove ingredients from the bowl and drop in the mint leaves. Add the meat to the marinade in a bowl or pan and marinate for up to 2 to 3 hours. Makes approximately 1 cup of marinade.

From the chef:

Have butcher clean the tenderloins completely of all silver skin. Place the tenderloins in the marinade for two to three hours. Before putting the tenderloins on a hot, well-seasoned grill, remove excess marinade from the meat. Turn while grilling, until desired temperature is reached. Use the excess marinade to baste the pork tenderloins. Remember to let the meat rest for 5 minutes before slicing.

Grilled Corn-on-the-Cob

6   ears of corn, cleaned all the
    way down to the kernels

    Large pot of boiling water

½   cup olive oil

¼   cup fresh herbs

    Salt and pepper to taste

Place the corn in the pot of boiling water and boil for 1½ minutes. Remove and set aside.

Prepare the marinade by combining the herbs and olive oil. Brush the corn with the olive oil mixture. Season with salt and pepper. Put the corn on the grill and grill until the corn starts to brown. Remove and serve.

From the chef:

There are many ways to grill corn, but this is a very good way to reheat leftover corn-on-the-cob. The texture of the corn may be a bit chewy, but the corn is nonetheless very tasty.

Makes 6 servings.

Grilled New Potatoes

6 small to medium red potatoes, cut in half with skins intact

9 tablespoons olive oil

3 cloves garlic, crushed

½ cup parsley, chopped

1 tablespoon fresh thyme

1 tablespoon fresh rosemary

1½ teaspoons paprika

Dash of cayenne

Salt and coarse black pepper to taste

Cook the potatoes in a pot of boiling salted water until the potatoes are nearly done. Remove from the water. Do not cool down, just set aside. Combine the rest of the ingredients in a mixing bowl. When the potatoes are cool enough to handle, place them on bamboo skewers and pour the marinade over the potatoes. Allow the potatoes to marinate for 20 minutes before grilling.

Makes approximately 1 cup of marinade.

From the chef:

When using bamboo skewers, soak them in water for at least 30 minutes to keep them from burning on the grill. Grill the potatoes white side down first to get those nice grill marks.

Roasted Sweet Peppers

1 *red pepper*

1 *yellow pepper*

1 *green pepper*

Roast the peppers over an open flame or under a broiler, charring evenly. Wrap the peppers in a paper towel. Place in a plastic bag for five minutes. Remove and rub the peppers with the paper towel to remove the skins.

Cut the peppers in half, removing the seeds and stems.

SUMMER

The idea for the Walt Garrison Rodeo Bar came from our out-of-state guests, who wanted a taste of the real Texas. They encouraged us to develop a casual spot where they could sample cowboy cuisine and listen to country/western music. With the help of our good friend Walt Garrison, retired Dallas Cowboys running back and rodeo star, we turned that great notion into a reality. Walt had only one request, and it was typical of his generosity: he asked that the North Texas Chapter of the Multiple Sclerosis Society serve as the restaurant's beneficiary in perpetuity. So, each year the MS Society draws on the Rodeo Bar to help it raise more than $1 million during the Walt Garrison All-Star Rodeo. It's a unique combination of free enterprise and philanthropy that is pure Texas.

Grilling, p. 57

WALT GARRISON RODEO BAR

Flank Steak Chili with Black Beans

Grilled Chicken and Chili Quesadillas

Crisp Tortillas with Fresh Tomato Salsa
and Guacamole

Smoked Brisket

Barbecued Pork Ribs

The Walt Garrison Rodeo Bar's Famous
Barbecue Sauce

Jalapeño Corn Bread Muffins

Sock-It-To-Me Cake

❖

(selected items pictured on opposite page)

Makes approximately 2 quarts.

Flank Steak Chili with Black Beans

2   *pounds flank steak, cut into ½-inch dice*

1   *teaspoon cumin powder*

¼   *teaspoon cayenne pepper*

1   *small onion, diced (small)*

1   *red bell pepper, diced (small)*

1   *green bell pepper, diced (small)*

4   *cloves garlic, crushed*

3   *tablespoons bacon fat*

2   *tablespoons salad oil*

3   *tablespoons masa harina*

1   *tablespoon all-purpose flour*

¼   *cup tomato paste*

¾   *cup ancho paste*

2   *small chipotle peppers, crushed*

1   *quart water*

2   *tablespoons honey*

2   *cups black beans, cooked (recipe on page 184)*

    Salt to taste

Season the flank steak with salt, cumin and cayenne pepper. This should be done ½ hour before cooking the meat.

Heat the bacon fat and salad oil in a 4-quart (or larger) soup pot. Add the flank steak and sauté for one minute. Add the red and green bell peppers, the onions and the garlic. Continue sautéing for 3 to 4 minutes. Reduce the heat and add the masa harina and flour. Continue cooking for 3 minutes, stirring well. Add the ancho paste, tomato paste and chipotle peppers. Then stir in the water. Increase the heat to a simmer and cook for 1 hour. Finish with the honey, salt and black beans.

From the chef:

If some of the ingredients can't be found, make the recipe without them. Creating new chili recipes is part of the fun.

Ancho Paste

5 ancho peppers
½ medium onion
3 cups water
1 clove garlic
1 jalapeño pepper

Soften the ancho peppers in a 350°F oven for one minute. Remove the stems and seeds. Combine all of the ingredients in a sauce pot and bring to a simmer. Cook until onions are translucent and the ancho peppers are soft. Pour mixture into a blender and blend until smooth. (A small amount of water may be necessary for blending.)

Makes 6 servings.

Grilled Chicken and Chili Quesadillas

12 nine-inch flour tortillas

4½ cups grated Monterey jack cheese

1 cup mild green chiles (canned), diced

4 grilled chicken breasts, diced (small)

3 cups uncooked spinach, chopped

¼ cup salad oil

Lay 6 of the flour tortillas on a work surface. Cover each with equal parts cheese. (Be sure to spread the cheese out to the edges.) Do the same with the spinach. Sprinkle each tortilla with the diced chicken and chiles. Cover with the remaining 6 tortillas and press down firmly.

Heat the salad oil in a Teflon-coated skillet over medium heat. Brown both sides of the quesadillas, then place in a preheated 350°F oven for approximately 3 to 5 minutes. Remove from the oven and cut into triangles. Serve with pico de gallo, salsa and guacamole.

Fresh Corn Tortilla Chips

There really is no substitute for freshly-made corn tortilla chips. So, you will probably want to make your own.

Purchase fresh corn tortillas from a Mexican food store. Cut them into triangles and keep covered. Heat peanut oil in a skillet to 300°F and carefully place chips in the hot oil. Fry until the bubbles stop, approximately 10 seconds. Remove from the oil and drain well on paper towels. Season with salt while chips are still warm.

From the chef:

The tortillas can be cut into any shape desired. We cut them into strips, deep fry them and use them as a garnish for tortilla soup and chili.

Makes 3 quarts.

Tomato Salsa

5   medium beefsteak tomatoes

1   can (16 ounces) whole peeled
    tomatoes

1   to 2 tablespoons chopped
    cilantro

1   medium onion

1   to 2 fresh jalapeño peppers

½   teaspoon crushed red pepper
    flakes

1   lime, juiced

    Salt and pepper to taste

Grind the ingredients through the small die of a meat grinder. (You may also use a food processor.) Chill well and serve cold.

From the chef:

Never touch your eyes while handling fresh jalapeño peppers. The peppers are hot and will burn your eyes. So wash hands well after touching them.

Guacamole

10 ripe avocados, halved, pitted, and skinned

1 beefsteak tomato, diced (small)

1 medium onion, diced (small)

2 jalapeño peppers, minced

1 bunch cilantro, chopped

Salt to taste

1 lemon, juiced

1 lime, juiced

Place avocados in a large mixing bowl, and mash by hand. Fold in the remaining ingredients. Season with salt.

From the chef:

If mashing avocados by hand isn't for you, use a spoon or potato masher. Add some of the avocado seeds to the finished product and cover with a wet paper towel to prevent browning.

Makes 8 to 12 servings.

Smoked Brisket

1   brisket (8 to 10) pounds

1   quart barbecue sauce

2   tablespoons chili powder

2   tablespoons cumin

1   tablespoon onion powder

2   tablespoons kosher salt

2   tablespoons coarse black
    pepper

Rub both sides of the brisket with dry spices; then marinate it for one hour.

While the brisket is marinating, prepare the charcoals. Give coals enough time to burn to approximately 80 percent gray. Soak some wood chips in water ahead of time; and, when the charcoals are very hot, scatter the chips among coals to create a smoker. After coating the brisket with barbecue sauce, put it on the grill. Cover the grill and smoke the brisket for 2 to 3 hours. Baste the brisket with barbecue sauce periodically. Add more charcoals as needed to keep the heat constant inside the grill.

Remove the brisket from the grill. Slice and serve.

From the chef:

At The Adolphus we have a smoker in the main kitchen. Every night the chefs put 8 briskets, averaging 10 pounds each, into the smoker. The briskets are smoked for 10 hours at 200°F with lots of mesquite wood chips. We use no special marinades or spices. The real secret is slow cooking and starting out with a fatty brisket.

If mesquite wood isn't available, try using other hardwoods such as apple, cherry or hickory.

Barbecued Pork Ribs

3 large pork spare ribs

2 tablespoons chili powder

2 tablespoons cumin

1 tablespoon onion powder

2 tablespoons kosher salt

2 tablespoons coarse black pepper

1 pint barbecue sauce

Heat oven to 350°F.

Simmer the pork ribs in a large pot of boiling, salted water for 20 minutes. Drain and discard the water. Rub both sides of the ribs with dry spices and, coat evenly with the barbecue sauce.

Prepare the charcoals by burning them until they become gray. Place the ribs on the grill grate and brush them with barbecue sauce as they cook.

From the chef:

The ribs are fully cooked when the meat begins to fall away from the bones.

Makes approximately 2 quarts.

Walt Garrison Rodeo Bar Barbecue Sauce

½   *cup brown sugar*

1   *tablespoon barbecue spice*

1   *teaspoon chili powder*

½   *teaspoon English mustard*

2   *cups tomato paste*

2   *cups ketchup*

¼   *cup steak sauce*

2   *tablespoons Worcestershire sauce*

   Dash liquid smoke

1   *rib celery, roughly chopped*

½   *medium onion, roughly chopped*

1   *small carrot, roughly chopped*

2   *cloves garlic*

1   *teaspoon beef base*

2   *tablespoons honey*

¼   *cup vinegar*

Place all of the ingredients in a large soup pot. Simmer for 1 to 1½ hours. When liquid becomes too thick, add water. This can be held for up to one month if wrapped and refrigerated.

From the chef:

This barbecue sauce is time-consuming, but it's well worth the effort. Prepare this recipe days in advance.

Jalapeño Corn Bread Muffins

1¼	cups sugar
4	teaspoons salt
3½	cups all-purpose flour
¼	cup baking powder
4	eggs
1	cup salad oil
2	cups milk
1	cup cornmeal
½	cup sliced jalapeño peppers, chopped

Combine sugar, salt and baking powder in a mixing bowl and blend. Gradually add eggs, one at a time, and mix until well incorporated. Add flour and cornmeal. Follow with milk, oil and jalapeños. Mix well.

Grease muffin tins and fill approximately ⅔ full. Bake at 350°F for 15 to 20 minutes, or until muffins are firm to the touch.

From the chef:

These muffins are great served warm. Experiment by adding different grated cheeses and chopped onions.

Makes one 9-inch cake.

Sock-It-To-Me Cake

1½   cups butter

3   cups sugar

3   eggs

1½   cups sour cream

1½   teaspoons vanilla

3   cups all-purpose flour

1½   teaspoons salt

1½   teaspoons baking powder

Cream butter and sugar until light and fluffy. Add eggs, sour cream and vanilla. Add dry ingredients and mix until well incorporated. Pour one half of the batter into a greased loaf pan. Sprinkle filling over the batter and top with remaining batter. Bake at 350°F for 1 hour or until a toothpick comes out clean when inserted into center of cake.

Filling

½   cup brown sugar

½   cup pecan pieces

¾   teaspoon cinnamon

Mix all ingredients together in a small bowl and reserve.

From the chef:

The end result is similar to a coffee cake. This is delicious served warm with a scoop of vanilla ice cream.

SUMMER

Summer in Dallas is very casual. The annual Cattle Baron's Ball starts the season off with a barbecue at one of the state's large ranches. People are in a picnic mood, and fresh cold seafood is often on the menu. Terrace parties at The Adolphus offer guests a delightful alfresco dining experience. Framed by skyscrapers, the urban setting is spectacular. There is usually a breeze sent up from the Gulf — Dallas imports its weather as well as its seafood — so early summer can be quite pleasant.

SEAFOOD

Assorted Domestic and Imported Caviars
with Toast and Condiments

Chilled Marinated Gulf Prawns
with Cocktail Sauce

Escabeche of Sturgeon with Olives and
Preserved Tomatoes on a Cucumber Salad

Crab and Avocado Cakes
with Spicy Aioli Dipping Sauce

Lobster Bisque

Pan-seared Soft-Shell Crabs
with Lemon Tartar Sauce

Fresh Peach and Ginger Pound Cake Parfaits

❖

(selected items pictured on page 88)

Makes 2 servings.

Assorted Domestic and Imported Caviars

1 ounce domestic caviar

1 ounce imported caviar

1½ tablespoons red onion, finely diced

2 hard cooked eggs, finely diced

1½ tablespoons capers

4 slices toasted white bread, crusts removed

2 tablespoons sour cream

Place caviar in small caviar servers or leave in original containers. Serve the condiments on the side.

From the chef:

Domestic caviars have become very popular in the last 5 years. The best is the American malossal which comes from a variety of American sturgeon, such as the hackleback, paddlefish or spoonbill. For imported caviar, the choices are beluga, ossetra and sevruga.

Chilled Marinated Gulf Prawns

12   *jumbo shrimp*

1½ *quarts water*

2   *cinnamon sticks*

3   *cloves garlic*

1   *jalapeño pepper, chopped*

4   *cloves*

1   *tablespoon pickling spice*

1   *teaspoon Old Bay seasoning*

    Kosher salt to taste

Combine all ingredients, except the shrimp, in a large pot filled with water. Bring to a boil and simmer for 2 minutes. Slowly add the shrimp and bring the water back to a boil. As soon as the water boils, turn the heat off. Let the shrimp remain in the liquid for 1 more minute. Remove the shrimp with half of the liquid. Put shrimp and half the liquid in a bowl and add a tray of ice. Chill shrimp before removing shells. Serve with cocktail sauce (recipe on page 203).

From the chef:

Letting the shrimp cool in the seasoned liquid will help retain the most flavor. They can be kept in this liquid for as long as a day. If the shrimp stay in the liquid any longer than a day, they may become too hot from the jalapeño.

Seafood, p. 85

Makes four 3-ounce servings.

Escabeche of Sturgeon

4   *three-ounce sturgeon fillets*

½   *cup green olives marinated in garlic oil and herbs, sliced*

½   *cup black Greek olives, sliced*

½   *medium onion, sliced*

3   *cloves garlic, crushed*

1   *shallot bulb*

¼   *cup diced fresh herbs (tarragon, thyme, whole bay leaf, chervil and cilantro)*

1   *jalapeño pepper, diced*

1   *cup preserved tomatoes*

2   *cups cucumber salad*

1   *cup extra virgin olive oil*

⅓   *cup champagne vinegar*

1   *tablespoon ketchup*

   Salt and pepper to taste

Optional ingredients:

   Julienne celery, carrots, leeks, snow peas and fresh peas

In a nonstick sauté pan, add a small amount of olive oil and quickly sauté the sturgeon on both sides. Place on a serving platter. After sautéing all the fish fillets, add the olives, onion, garlic, shallot, herbs, jalapeños and any of the optional ingredients. Sauté for 30 seconds and add the vinegar and ketchup. Remove from pan and place in a stainless steel bowl. Slowly add the remaining olive oil. Pour over the fish and marinate for 24 hours. Season with salt and pepper.

Right before serving, spoon a small amount of the tomato preserves on top of the fish. Pour a little of the marinade all around the fish. Serve with a small portion of cucumber salad.

From the chef:

Any type of fish can be used. This recipe is served cold; however, the vegetable mix can be spooned over hot fish, too.

Preserved Tomatoes

30 Roma tomatoes, peeled and seeded

½ cup fresh garlic, diced and packed in oil

½ cup olive oil

Line a baking sheet with aluminum foil and brush the foil with the garlic oil. Using only the fleshy pieces, place the tomatoes on top of the foil and brush with garlic oil. Bake the tomatoes in a 250°F oven for 1 to 1½ hours. Baste them frequently with the garlic oil. Remove from the oven and pack in a jar with olive oil.

Makes about 1 cup of tomatoes.

Cucumber Salad

6 large cucumbers, seeded and thinly sliced

3 tablespoons salt

⅓ cup red wine vinegar

1 red onion, thinly sliced

Put the sliced cucumbers and onions in a stainless steel bowl and cover with salt. Mix well; refrigerate for 2 hours. Rinse well under running water and drain. Add the red wine vinegar and refrigerate. Serve cold.

Makes 2 cups.

Makes 6 small pancakes.

Crab and Avocado Cakes

1   cup jumbo lump crab meat,
    cleaned of all shells

½   cup mayonnaise

2   slices of fresh white bread,
    crusts removed

1   tablespoon fresh chives

1   teaspoon chopped parsley

½   lemon, seeds removed for
    juicing

    Splash of Worcestershire
    sauce

    Splash of Tabasco

1   large avocado, meat removed
    just before mixing

¼   teaspoon cumin

¼   teaspoon cayenne

¼   teaspoon chili powder

    Salt and white pepper to
    taste

1   cup all-purpose flour

½   cup salad or peanut oil for
    frying

Combine all ingredients, except the oil and flour, in a stainless steel bowl and mix well. Marinate crab mixture for one hour. Rub a little flour on your hand and form the crab mix into small pancakes. Put each crab cake in flour and dredge well. Heat the oil in a skillet and carefully place the crab cakes in the hot oil. Brown evenly on both sides. Remove the crab cakes from the skillet and place on paper towels. Serve warm with aioli dipping sauce (recipe on following page).

From the chef:

Crab cakes have been a very popular menu item for sometime now. The recipes continue to evolve, with a variety of foods being added to the basic crab mix. Here in the Southwest where avocados are plentiful, that pulpy green fruit is often paired with crab meat. Mashed yams are another good choice.

Aioli Sauce

3	egg yolks
¾-1	cup olive oil
1	clove garlic
	Cayenne pepper to taste
	Salt and white pepper

Put all ingredients, except the olive oil, in a blender or food processor. Blend for 5 seconds. Turn the processor or blender to medium speed and slowly pour in the olive oil.

Check seasonings and refrigerate for 1 hour before serving.

From the chef:

Aioli now comes in a variety of forms, such as mint aioli, basil aioli, and yellow pepper aioli. However, aioli actually refers to a basic mayonnaise recipe that includes garlic.

Makes 6 to 8 servings.

Lobster Bisque

2   1¼-pound lobsters, meat removed and shells reserved

1   rib celery, finely diced

½   onion, finely diced

1   carrot, finely diced

3   cloves garlic, crushed

¼   cup vermouth

2   tablespoons tomato paste

4   cups chicken stock

2   cups heavy cream

2   tablespoons tarragon

1   tablespoon parsley

1   tablespoon flour

1   tablespoon butter

¼   cup sherry

¼   cup Cognac

½   cup olive oil

Salt and pepper to taste

Using a large roasting pan, heat the olive oil over medium high heat. Put in the lobster shells and brown. Add the celery, onion, carrot and garlic. When vegetables start to brown, pour in the vermouth, sherry and Cognac. The liquors may ignite, so be careful. (The flames help remove the alcohol from the liquors.) Reduce the liquors until they are almost dry. Add tomato paste, chicken stock and heavy cream. Bring to a simmer and cook for 15 minutes.

Combine the flour and butter. Add this to the pot along with the herbs. Let the bisque simmer for an additional 20 to 30 minutes. Strain through a fine sieve and season with salt and pepper. Keep hot until ready to serve.

From the chef:

The hotel makes great quantities of bisque everyday. It takes time to make it, but bisque can be made in advance and frozen for later use. The finished product is very smooth and velvety. Use the reserved lobster meat in the soup cups as a garnish.

Pan-seared Soft-Shell Crabs

8   soft-shell crabs
1   cup all-purpose flour
¼   cup olive oil
    Salt and pepper to taste
2½ cups tartar sauce
    (recipe below)

Clean soft-shell crabs by removing the lungs (under the top shell, both sides) and the flap underneath. Rinse the crabs under cold running water and pat dry. Combine the flour, salt, and pepper. Coat the crabs completely with the flour mixture; dust off any excess flour.

Heat the olive oil in a skillet over medium heat and sauté the crabs on both sides. Remove them from the skillet and place in a 350°F oven for 5 minutes. Serve the crabs on a large platter with the tartar sauce on the side.

Tartar Sauce

1   cup mayonnaise
½   cup chopped gherkins or
    pickles
¼   cup capers
    Juice of 1 lemon
    Splash Worcestershire sauce
    Splash Tabasco
    Salt and pepper

Combine all the ingredients in a mixing bowl and marinate for 1 hour.

Makes 2½ cups.

Makes 6 to 8 servings.

Peach and Ginger Pound Cake Parfait

½ gallon vanilla ice cream

1 loaf ginger pound cake
(recipe on following page)

10 – 12 fresh peaches

1½ cups raspberry coulis

Whipped cream (optional)

Mint sprigs (optional)

Slice peaches into eighths and set aside. Cut pound cake into one-inch cubes.

Using large parfait glasses, layer as follows: one scoop of ice cream, two tablespoons raspberry coulis and a few slices of peaches topped with pound cake. Repeat layers and top with whipped cream and peaches. Garnish with sprigs of mint.

Raspberry Coulis

2 pints fresh raspberries

Simple syrup

Lime or lemon juice

Purée raspberries in a blender or food processor. Add simple syrup and juice to taste. Strain through a fine sieve to remove seeds.

Simple Syrup

½ cup water

¾ cup sugar

¼ teaspoon vanilla extract

Bring sugar and water to a boil in a saucepan. Cool and add vanilla.

Makes 6 to 8 servings.

Ginger Pound Cake

1	cup shortening
2	cups sugar
4	eggs
1	teaspoon vanilla
3	cups sifted cake flour
¾	teaspoon salt
½	teaspoon baking powder
1	cup buttermilk
1½	teaspoons ground ginger

Cream shortening and sugar until light and fluffy. Add eggs one at a time, beating well after each addition. Pour in vanilla. Sift dry ingredients into creamed mixture, alternating with buttermilk.

Pour cake batter into a 9" × 4" × 4" greased loaf pan. Bake at 300°F for approximately 1 hour, or until toothpick comes out clean when inserted into center of the cake.

SEAFOOD   97

SUMMER

There's something about dining outdoors that adds a certain spice to whatever is served. At The Adolphus many of our guests reserve the Terrace Suites so they can entertain their friends alfresco. These private red-tiled patios, with their topiaries and wrought iron furniture, provide the perfect settings for intimate luncheons, cozy afternoon teas, and elegant dinner parties. The menu is always light, featuring perhaps a fresh tossed salad with thinly sliced chicken, and the conversation is too — often touching on what Dallas Summer Musicals stars were spotted in the hotel's lobby living room. Was that Sandy Duncan and Tommy Tune behind those dark glasses?

SUMMER

ALFRESCO

Warm Crab Dip in New Potato Cups

Grilled Chicken Salad Tossed in a
Honey Mustard Vinaigrette

Candy Apples

Apple Pie

❖

(selected items pictured on page 87)

Makes 12 servings.

Warm Crab Dip in New Potato Cups

1   cup crab meat, shells removed

2   tablespoons white wine

½   cup cream cheese

1   tablespoon lemon juice

1   clove garlic, finely diced

2   tablespoons chives, finely diced

½   teaspoon Worcestershire sauce

    Splash of Tabasco sauce

    Salt and pepper to taste

6   small new potatoes

1   teaspoon paprika

Bring a pot of water to a boil and cook the new potatoes in their jackets until they are fully cooked. Remove and cool. When potatoes are cool enough to handle, cut them in half. Scoop a small amount out of each half. Line the potatoes up evenly on a baking sheet and set aside.

In a food processor fitted with a metal blade, combine the crab meat, white wine, cream cheese, lemon juice, garlic, chives, Worcestershire sauce, Tabasco sauce, salt and pepper. Blend well. Remove the mixture from the food processor. Using a small spoon, put a small amount into each of the potatoes. Top off with paprika and bake in a 350°F oven for 6 to 8 minutes. Serve warm.

Makes 6 servings.

Grilled Chicken Salad

6   chicken breasts, skin and
    bones removed

1   head radicchio

1   head red oak leaf lettuce

2   pieces Belgian endive

1   cup soya vinaigrette

½   cup whole cashews

3   carrots cut into long pieces

¼   cup olive oil

Clean the lettuces and cut into bite size pieces. Soak them in ice water for 20 minutes. Place in a colander and drain well.

Marinate the chicken breasts in the soya vinaigrette (recipe on following page) for 2 to 3 hours. Remove and drain well. Heat a skillet with some of the olive oil and cook the chicken breasts thoroughly. After they have cooled, cut each breast into thin slices.

Toss the salad greens with the honey mustard vinaigrette (recipe on following page) and arrange even amounts on 6 platters. Place the chicken breast slices on top of the salad greens. Garnish with the carrot slices and cashews.

Honey Mustard Dressing

1   cup mayonnaise
2   tablespoons Pommery
    mustard
1½ tablespoons honey
½   lemon, juiced
    Salt and pepper to taste

Combine mayonnaise, mustard, honey, lemon juice and salt and pepper in a small mixing bowl. Chill well.

Makes 1 cup.

Soya Vinaigrette

½   cup soy sauce
¼   cup rice vinegar
2   cloves garlic
2   sprigs green onions, finely
    diced
½   cup chicken broth
1   tablespoon ginger
1   tablespoon brown sugar
¼   cup sesame oil
½   cup salad oil

In a blender, mix the soy sauce, vinegar, garlic, chicken broth, ginger and brown sugar. While the blender is running, slowly add the oils until the vinaigrette thickens. Turn the blender off and add in the green onions.

Makes 2 cups.

From the chef:

This is the most popular salad at The Adolphus. We serve it in the Bistro, the Rodeo Bar, and in guest room dining.

Guests often request it when they host a private luncheon on the terrace of a suite. Try serving the dressing on the side — it makes a great dip!

Candy Apples

10 medium apples
2½ cups sugar
½ cup light corn syrup
½ cup water
1 teaspoon vanilla
1 teaspoon red food coloring
1 drop of cinnamon oil

Insert wooden sticks in the blossom end of the apples.

Combine sugar, syrup, water, vanilla and coloring. Cook without stirring to hard-crack stage or 380°F on a candy thermometer.

Remove from heat and dip apples in the hot mixture. Cool on wax paper.

Apple Pie

Crust:

5½	cups pastry or all-purpose flour
2	cups vegetable shortening
3½	tablespoons sugar
1	tablespoon salt
1	cup cold water

Filling:

8	Granny Smith apples, cored and sliced
¾	cup sugar
1	teaspoon cinnamon
¼	cup pecans
2	tablespoons butter
1	egg, beaten (to use for wash)

To make the crust, sift flour, sugar, and salt together in a large mixing bowl. Cut in shortening until mixture resembles fine crumbs. Pour in water and mix until dough clings together. Refrigerate dough for approximately one hour before rolling out crust. Divide dough in half and roll out each to cover a 9-inch pie pan. Place one piece in the pan.

For the filling, combine sugar and cinnamon. Mix carefully with apples and pecans. Place in pie crust and dot with butter. Brush edges of pie crust with egg. Cover with the second piece of pie dough. Press edges together to seal the pie. Make a small hole in the center to allow steam to escape. Brush top of pie with remaining egg mixture and bake at 400°F for approximately 40 to 50 minutes.

Picnic, p. 109 and
Texas-OU Tailgating, p. 119

SUMMER

Whether it's in town or in the country, a gourmet picnic — or as the French would say a pique-nique — is the perfect way to celebrate in the summer sunshine. Dallas has many beautiful parks throughout the city; and, although we don't do a great deal of outside catering, we sometimes prepare a picnic basket for a special outing. In it go some of our richest gourmet treasures, including crusty French bread with cheese and pâté, crab picwiches, and luscious fresh fruit compotes. And what would a Texas picnic be without a chilled pitcher of Sangria!

PICNIC

Fruit Compote

Jumbo Lump Crab Picwich

Country Fried Chicken

French Bread with Cheese and Pâté

Sangria

Minted Iced Tea

❖

(selected items pictured on page 105)

Makes 6 to 12 servings.

Fruit Compote

2 apples, cored and sliced

2 pears, cored and sliced

1 orange, peeled and diced

1 pint strawberries, cut in half (stems removed)

½ pint blueberries

½ pint raspberries

1 cup green and red grapes cut in half (lengthwise)

¼ cup dried apricots

¼ cup dried figs

¼ cup dried banana chips

¼ cup fresh mint

¾ cup apple juice

Juice of one lemon

In a large mixing bowl, combine all of the ingredients. Marinate for one hour before serving.

From the chef:

So often fruit salad is served plain, and some of the fruits have not ripened thoroughly. Since it includes fruit juices, this recipe enhances the flavor of the natural fruits. The dried fruits add an interesting texture. This is a basic recipe to which you can add your favorite fruit salad ingredients.

Jumbo Lump Crab Picwich

1   *pound jumbo lump crab meat, shells removed*

3/4   *cup mayonnaise*

    Juice of one lemon

1½   *tablespoons toasted almonds, thinly sliced*

1   *small bunch red grapes, cut in half (lengthwise)*

    Splash of Cognac

1   *sprig green onion, finely diced*

    Salt and pepper to taste

1   *long loaf French bread*

In a stainless steel mixing bowl, combine the crab, mayonnaise, lemon juice, almonds, grapes and green onions. Carefully toss these ingredients together, so the crab does not break up too much. Pour in a small amount of Cognac. Salt and pepper to taste. Serve the crab salad either inside 2 pieces of French bread or on the side as a dip.

From the chef:

The sweetness of the grapes and Cognac and the crunchiness of the almonds pair well with the fresh crab meat.

Makes 4 servings.

Country Fried Chicken

1 *3½-pound whole chicken, cut into 8 pieces*

2 *cups all-purpose flour*

4 *cloves garlic, crushed*

2 *tablespoons paprika*

½ *teaspoon cayenne*

1 *teaspoon salt*

1 *teaspoon coarse ground black pepper*

2 *cups buttermilk*

   Splash of Tabasco sauce

½ *teaspoon celery salt*

2 *quarts peanut or safflower oil for frying*

Mix together the garlic, buttermilk and Tabasco sauce in a large mixing bowl. Marinate the chicken pieces in this mixture for 20 minutes.

In another large mixing bowl, combine the flour, paprika, cayenne, salt, pepper and celery salt. Coat the chicken pieces with the flour mixture. Repeat process by returning the floured chicken pieces to the buttermilk mixture. Flour chicken pieces a second time. Refrigerate the coated chicken pieces for 20 minutes. While the chicken is chilling, heat the frying oil until it starts to bubble when a chicken piece is submerged. Fry the chicken until it turns a golden brown. Put the chicken pieces on a cookie sheet. Check the chicken to make sure it is done. If the chicken is still a little pink inside, finish cooking it in a 325°F oven.

Let the chicken cool at room temperature before refrigerating.

From the chef:

Save the chicken grease in an old coffee can and place it in the freezer. Once the can is filled, it can easily be discarded.

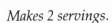

French Bread with Cheese and Pâté

1   long loaf French bread

6   ounces ripened brie

6   ounces ripened Camembert

1   medium size bunch red
    grapes

1   large ripened pear

1   large firm, red apple

6   ounces country pâté

1   small jar Pommery mustard

1   small jar gherkins

1   bread knife

This recipe requires you to use your own creativity. Pack all of the ingredients in a wicker picnic basket. Bring along a checkered tablecloth or tartan picnic blanket. Combine the ingredients in an imaginative and interesting way. The proof of this recipe will be in how long your guests linger after the last bite of pâté.

From the chef:

Without a doubt, these ingredients mixed with good friends are the essence of a perfect summer picnic. The ingredients can be bought at a local gourmet food store; the friends . . . well, you're on your own there.

Makes 6 one-cup servings.

Sangria

¼ cup grenadine

1 quart white wine

12 ounces Seven-Up

1 orange, thinly sliced

6 strawberries

½ pint raspberries

6 mint leaves

Large pitcher of ice

Pour grenadine, white wine and Seven-Up over the ice. Drop in the orange slices, strawberries and raspberries. Stir well. Chill for a few minutes in the refrigerator or freezer. Pour into serving glasses. Garnish each glass with a mint sprig. (There should be a strawberry in each glass.)

From the chef:

Sangria can also be made with red wine. Try substituting champagne or club soda for Seven-Up. These subtle changes will alter the flavor but not the outcome.

Minted Iced Tea

4 cups of tea

10 mint sprigs

Sugar to taste

While making the tea, steep with 10 mint leaves. Remove tea bags and mint. Add sugar. Chill and serve over ice.

From the chef:

Try using a flavored tea with this recipe.

AUTUMN

AT THE ADOLPHUS

AUTUMN

From the moment Texas and Oklahoma
first met on the gridiron, a spirited rivalry
took root that has kept both sides cheering
for decades. More than once The Adolphus
has found itself in the midst of the
scrimmaging (in the old days, we are told,
fans celebrated by hurling hotel furniture
out of the windows!). From the culinary
sidelines, it's just the right time for picnics
and tailgate parties. No matter who wins,
the simple fare always gets a cheer.

TEXAS-OU TAILGATING

Sweet Potato Chips and Regular Potato Chips

Regular Hoagie with the Works

Potato Salad

Cole Slaw

Marinated Vegetables

Tuna-Pasta Salad

Chocolate-Chocolate Cake

❖

(selected items pictured on page 106)

Sweet Potato Chips and Regular Potato Chips

2   sweet potatoes, yams or
    regular potatoes

2   cups peanut oil

    Kosher salt (coarse grind)

Slice the potatoes into ¹⁄₁₆-inch slices and place in cold water. In a heavy saucepan or small home fryer, heat the oil to 350°F. Pat sliced potatoes dry with a towel. If using a saucepan, drop one slice into hot oil to test temperature. If potato slice begins to bubble and float, oil is hot enough. Fry the potatoes in small batches until they are golden brown. Place the chips on a small sheet pan lined with paper towels. Season while they are still warm.

From the chef:

This recipe can be used for any type of potato. Seasoning depends on personal taste. Homemade potato chips disappear by the handful, so make plenty of them.

Regular Hoagie (with or without the works)

1 loaf French bread, approximately 16 inches long

½ pound sliced salami

½ pound sliced boiled ham

½ pound sliced cappacolla

¼ pound sliced mozzarella cheese

¼ pound sliced provolone cheese

1 head iceberg lettuce, shredded

1 sliced tomato

1 sliced onion

½ cup olive oil

⅛ cup red wine vinegar

2 tablespoons sweet cherry peppers

1 tablespoon hot cherry peppers

1 tablespoon dry oregano

1 tablespoon dry basil

Without cutting all the way through the bread, slice lengthwise and spread open. Pour the olive oil in a slow, steady stream over the bread. Line one side of the bread with the salami and the other side with the boiled ham. Place the cappacolla down the center of the bread. Repeat the process with cheeses, putting the cheeses on one side and then the other. Then place the shredded lettuce down the center and top with the tomatoes, onions, and sweet and hot cherry peppers. Sprinkle the entire sandwich with the vinegar, dried oregano and basil.

From the chef:

The "works" can include your favorite sandwich fixings. Some people like to add mayonnaise and fried onions. Many prefer to serve hoagies warm; these are called grinders. This particular hoagie recipe — also known as a "hero" or "submarine"— comes from Philadelphia where they originated.

Potato Salad

8   medium red potatoes

⅛   cup white vinegar

1   small can chicken broth

1   tablespoon brown mustard

1   bunch green onions, chopped

1   cup mayonnaise

    Salt and pepper

Bring unpeeled potatoes to a boil in a large pot. Cook until a skewer inserted into potato goes all the way through. Remove from the water and cool at room temperature. As soon as potatoes can be handled comfortably, peel and cut into large dice. While still warm, sprinkle with vinegar and set aside at room temperature for 10 minutes. Add the rest of the ingredients and chill in the refrigerator for one day before serving.

From the chef:

The addition of chicken broth may make the salad appear too watery. But cooking potatoes in their jackets helps retain their natural starch; during the chilling period, the salad will thicken. Always stir the salad and check the seasoning before serving.

Pizza, p. 123

Cole Slaw

2   heads green cabbage, grated

¼   head red cabbage, grated

1   large carrot, grated

1   small red onion, diced

1   bunch green onions, diced

Combine all of the dressing ingredients in a small mixing bowl. After preparing the vegetables and placing them in a salad bowl, pour the dressing over them and toss. Marinate the cole slaw for at least 1 hour.

From the chef:

It is important to mix the dressing repeatedly to ensure that all the flavors are incorporated before it is added to the vegetables.

Dressing

2   cups mayonnaise

½   cup red wine vinegar

¼   cup horseradish

1   tablespoon salt

Roasted Acorn Squash Soup, p. 133

Makes 12 servings.

Marinated Vegetables

1   head broccoli

2   carrots

1   pound asparagus

2   red peppers

2   yellow peppers

1   large summer squash

1   pint cherry tomatoes

1   red onion

Cut the broccoli into flowerets, the carrots into strips, and the asparagus into bite-size pieces. Blanch the broccoli, carrots and asparagus separately in boiling, salted water. Remove from boiling water and shock in ice water. Remove from ice water and set aside.

Then cut the peppers into large dice, the red onions into slices, the cherry tomatoes in half and the summer squash into strips.

After placing all of the vegetables in a mixing bowl, pour the marinade (recipe on following page) over them. Marinate the vegetables in the refrigerator for at least 2 hours.

Vinaigrette Marinade for Marinated Vegetables

½   cup red wine vinegar

2¼ cups olive oil

1   shallot bulb, crushed

2   cloves garlic, crushed

1   teaspoon brown mustard

1   tablespoon chives, finely diced

1   tablespoon parsley, finely diced

1   teaspoon thyme, finely diced

Salt and pepper to taste

Combine all ingredients, except the olive oil, in a stainless steel mixing bowl. Using a wire whisk, slowly add the olive oil in a slow, steady stream until it is well incorporated.

From the chef:

You can use whatever vegetables are on hand. Consider adding diced pepperoni or diced chicken breast. Fresh herbs, such as basil and dill, will also enhance the flavor.

Makes 12 to 16 servings.

Tuna–Pasta Salad

5   cans (6¾ ounces each) tuna

8   ounces cooked pasta shells

2   cups mayonnaise

6   hard boiled eggs, sliced and diced

3   ribs celery, diced (small)

1   medium onion, diced (small)

Garlic salt to taste

White pepper to taste

Mix all of the ingredients together in a stainless steel mixing bowl. Let the mixture marinate in the refrigerator for at least 2 hours.

From the chef:

To add more color to this recipe, include diced pimento or some English peas. This salad can be used as a light entree with fresh fruit.

Chocolate-Chocolate Cake

1¾   cups sifted cake flour
1½   cups sugar
 1   teaspoon baking soda
 1   teaspoon salt
½   cup cocoa
½   cup shortening
 1   cup buttermilk
 2   eggs

Sift cake flour, sugar, soda, salt and cocoa into a bowl. Add shortening and ⅔ cup buttermilk. Beat with electric mixer on medium speed for two minutes. Add remaining buttermilk and eggs. Beat for another two minutes.

Pour batter into a greased 10" cake pan. Bake at 350°F for approximately 30 minutes, or until a toothpick comes out clean when inserted into the middle of the cake. Cool.

Slice cake into 3 even layers. Ice with chocolate cream cheese icing.

Chocolate Cream Cheese Icing

1½   pounds cream cheese
 2   sticks soft butter
 3   cups sifted powdered sugar
 3   cups chocolate ganache

Place all four ingredients in a mixing bowl. Beat for 1 to 2 minutes, until icing is smooth and spreadable.

Chocolate Ganache

30   ounces semisweet chocolate
1½   cups heavy cream

Bring cream to a boil in a saucepan. Remove from heat and stir in chocolate until all of the chocolate is incorporated. Cool for 2 hours.

Makes 3 cups.

AUTUMN

Reminiscent of holiday meals taken
around family dining room tables,
Thanksgiving in The Bistro is warm
and inviting, combining early
American traditions with current
culinary trends. The day often finds
Dallas residents seated beside our
international guests, who are often
experiencing for the first time a taste
of America's history.

THANKSGIVING FEAST

Spicy Texas Pecans

Roasted Acorn Squash Soup with
Cheddar Cheese Straws and Apple Cider Cream

Stuffed Breast of Turkey with
Fresh Sage and Sausage Stuffing

Cranberry Pumpkin Chutney

Pan-Fried Brussels Sprouts with Bacon and Onions

Jalapeño Corn Bread Muffins

Sweet Potato Pancakes

Chocolate Maple Pecan Pie

❖

(Squash Soup pictured on page 124)

Makes 4 cups.

Spicy Texas Pecans

4   *cups pecan halves*

¼   *cup butter*

Splash Worcestershire sauce

Splash Tabasco

Pinch cumin

Pinch chili powder

Pinch garlic salt

Kosher salt to taste

After melting the butter, add it to the Worcestershire sauce, Tabasco, cumin, chili powder and garlic salt. Toss the pecans in the butter mixture and spread the nuts evenly on a Teflon cookie sheet. Place in a preheated 325°F oven for 15 minutes.

From the chef:

While the pecans are in the oven, stir them a couple of times. When they are done, remove them from the oven and cool at room temperature.

Roasted Acorn Squash Soup

2 cloves garlic, crushed

1 whole shallot, finely diced

1 medium onion, diced (medium)

6 pieces smoked bacon, diced (small)

5 medium acorn squash

2 Idaho potatoes, 120 count, peeled and diced (large)

1 quart chicken stock

3½ ounces maple syrup

1 cup apple cider

1 quart heavy cream

1 tablespoon fresh thyme

Salt and white pepper to taste

3 ounces clarified butter

2 ounces salad oil

Rub the acorn squash with the salad oil and place on a sheet pan. Roast for approximately 5 minutes in a 350°F oven. (The squash will soften when they are cooked all the way through.) Remove from the oven and cool. Take off the outer skins and inner seeds, and save just the pulp of the squash.

In a heavy-bottomed 2-gallon saucepan, heat the clarified butter and sauté the garlic, onion, bacon and shallots. Sauté until the bacon is ¾ done. Pour in the apple cider and chicken stock. Bring to a boil and add the potatoes. After simmering for 5 minutes, add the squash, maple syrup and fresh thyme. Continue to cook until the potatoes are done. Season with salt and white pepper. Pour in the heavy cream.

After removing the soup from the stove, blend it with either an emulsion blender or a large kitchen blender. Adjust seasoning. Reheat and serve.

From the chef:

Set aside the nicest squash in which to serve the soup. Cut straight across the top of the squash and remove the seeds and membrane; then cut straight across the bottom so the squash will stand straight. Serving the soup in the squash shells will greatly enhance its presentation.

Cheddar Cheese Straws

1 puff pastry sheet, 6" x 9"
1 cup grated cheddar cheese
   Paprika
1 egg for wash

Mark puff pastry sheet into 1-inch strips. After brushing with egg wash, sprinkle with paprika and cover with cheddar cheese. Cut into strips. Starting at each end, simultaneously twist each strip two or three times and roll lightly with hands. Lay each strip on a paper-lined cookie sheet, pressing the two ends firmly on the paper. Bake at 375°F for approximately 15 minutes.

From the chef:

Garnishing the soup with the cheddar cheese straws eliminates the need for crackers or bread. Make plenty — your guests will ask for more!

Apple Cider Cream

2 cups apple cider
½ cup heavy cream

In a saucepan, reduce the apple cider to a half cup. Chill in the refrigerator.

Whip the heavy cream until it forms soft peaks. Then add the chilled apple cider.

Place a small dollop of the cider cream on top of each serving of soup.

Stuffed Breast of Turkey

1   *five pound boneless breast of turkey, uncooked*

2½ *pounds sage and sausage stuffing (recipe follows)*

    Butcher's twine

    Salt and pepper to taste

    Butter or olive oil to baste turkey breast

Fresh Sage and Sausage Stuffing

2   *pounds Italian sausage*

1   *small onion, finely diced*

3   *cloves garlic, finely diced*

1   *loaf white bread, crust removed, diced (large)*

¼   *cup fresh sage, finely diced*

1½ *cups chicken stock*

2   *eggs*

1   *tablespoon dry thyme*

    Salt and pepper to taste

2   *tablespoons olive oil*

Cook the sausage over medium heat in a heavy skillet until completely cooked. After draining the grease thoroughly, remove the sausage from the skillet and reserve. Discard the grease.

In the same skillet, heat the olive oil and add the onion and garlic. Sauté for 1 minute. Add the sausage and mix well. Remove the sausage mixture from the skillet and place it in a mixing bowl. Stir in the remaining ingredients. Check the seasoning; add more dried spices if needed. Cool completely before stuffing the turkey breast.

Place the boneless breast of turkey on a cutting board. Remove and discard the skin. Cover the top of the breast with plastic wrap and flatten the breast with a meat mallet. Flatten to a 1-inch thickness. After removing the plastic wrap, season the breast with salt and pepper.

Spread the stuffing over the entire breast and roll it up like a jelly roll. Tie it with butcher's twine and rub the turkey roll with butter or olive oil. Roast in a 350°F oven for 45 minutes.

From the chef:

Oven temperatures vary from oven to oven, so it is difficult to set an exact roasting time. However, you can determine if the turkey is done by sticking a skewer in the center of the turkey roast. If the juices run out clear, the roast is done.

Makes approximately 8 servings.

Cranberry Pumpkin Chutney

1   *pound pumpkin, seeded and diced (large)*

1   *pound fresh cranberries*

3½ *cups brown sugar*

½   *cup cranberry juice*

½   *cup lemon juice*

½   *small onion, diced (medium)*

½   *cup small raisins*

1   *tablespoon fresh ginger, grated*

½   *teaspoon ground cinnamon*

½   *teaspoon ground nutmeg*

¼   *cup white vinegar*

Combine all of the ingredients in a large saucepan.

Cover and bring to a boil, stirring occasionally. Boil for 5 minutes. Remove cover and simmer until 95 percent of the liquid has evaporated.

From the chef:

This dish can be served either hot or cold. So, serve it hot the first day and cold the rest of the week. The taste improves with time.

Pan-Fried Brussels Sprouts

1½ *pound brussels sprouts*

1 *pound bacon, diced*

1 *small white onion, finely diced*

1 *tablespoon butter*

   Salt and pepper to taste

Bring a large pot of salted water to a boil. Add fresh brussels sprouts and simmer until the sprouts can be pierced with a paring knife. Remove from the pot and place in an ice-water bath to stop the cooking process. Strain from the ice bath after 10 or 12 minutes. Cut each sprout in half and reserve in a cold place.

While the sprouts are boiling, begin frying the diced bacon slowly over medium heat. When the bacon is ¾ cooked, add the onion. Sauté together until thoroughly cooked. Remove from pan, strain and reserve.

When ready to serve, heat a sauté pan over a medium high flame and add the butter. Then sauté the sprouts, bacon and onion until they are thoroughly heated. Season with salt and pepper. Serve immediately.

Jalapeño Corn Bread Muffins

1¼ cups sugar

4 teaspoons salt

3½ cups all-purpose flour

¼ cup baking powder

4 eggs

1 cup salad oil

2 cups milk

1 cup cornmeal

½ cup sliced jalapeño peppers, chopped

Combine sugar, salt and baking powder in a mixing bowl and blend. Gradually add eggs, one at a time, and mix until well incorporated. Add flour and corn meal. Follow with milk, oil and jalapeños. Mix well.

Grease muffin tins and fill approximately ⅔ full. Bake at 350°F for 15 to 20 minutes, or until muffins are firm to the touch.

From the chef:

These muffins are great served warm. Experiment by adding different grated cheeses and chopped onions.

Sweet Potato Pancakes

3   *large sweet potatoes, scrubbed clean*

¼   *cup fresh chives, finely chopped*

2   *eggs*

    Salt and pepper to taste

    Olive oil for sautéing

Grate the sweet potatoes into a stainless steel mixing bowl. Add the rest of the ingredients and let rest in the refrigerator for 10 minutes.

Heat some olive oil in a Teflon-coated skillet over medium high heat. Remove the potato mixture from the refrigerator. Using a spoon, place one spoonful at a time in the skillet. Brown completely on one side before turning. Brown the second side.

If you prefer, you can finish the potato pancakes in the oven. Set the oven at 325°F and bake for 10 minutes. This will keep them warm before serving.

Makes one 9" pie.

Chocolate Maple Pecan Pie

1½ cups maple syrup

6 eggs

¾ cup sugar

⅓ cup butter, melted

2 cups pecan pieces

3 ounces bitter chocolate, melted

1 unbaked 9" pie shell

Combine syrup, eggs, sugar, butter and melted chocolate in a medium mixing bowl. Mix until smooth. Sprinkle in pecan pieces. Pour into a pie shell and bake at 350°F for 30 to 40 minutes. Center of pie should be firm to the touch. Cool before serving.

Comfort Food from The Bistro, p. 145
and *Iced In*, p. 189

AUTUMN

The Bistro's culinary diversity includes hearty comfort food, just the right dishes to take the edge off of crisp October evenings. The authors who stay with us during their fall book tours find this regional home-style cooking a welcome change. Many are away from their families for weeks on end, and they find these simple menus charming and delicious. They also appreciate the personal touches for which The Adolphus has become famous: quilted comforters, fresh cut flowers, and welcoming amenities tailored to individual tastes.

Comfort Food from The Bistro

Sweet Texas Corn Chowder

Romaine Leaves Tossed in a Caesar Cream
with Baked Croutons

Chicken-Fried Steak with Cream Gravy

Mashed Potatoes with Garlic and Horseradish

Harvester Beans with Bacon and Onions

Multi-Grain Rolls

Ginger Applesauce Cake

❖

(selected items pictured on page 141)

Makes 12 one-cup servings.

Sweet Texas Corn Chowder

Preparing the stock:

> *Kernels cut from 6 ears fresh corn, cobs reserved*

- 1 *onion, rough chopped*
- 1 *green bell pepper, rough chopped*
- 1 *tablespoon butter*
- 1 *sprig thyme*
- 1 *sprig parsley*
- 3 *quarts chicken stock*

To finish:

- 10 *strips bacon, diced*
- 1 *onion, diced*
- 1 *red bell pepper, diced*
- 1 *green bell pepper, diced*
  Kernels from 6 ears fresh corn
- 1 *cup flour*
- 2 *cups heavy cream*
- 1 *tablespoon salt*
- 1 *teaspoon white pepper*
- 1 *teaspoon fresh thyme*
- 1 *cup cooked wild rice*
- 1 *cup cooked chicken, diced*

Gently sauté corn cobs, onion and pepper in butter over medium heat for 5 minutes. Add thyme, parsley and chicken stock. Simmer until liquid is reduced by ⅓. Strain and reserve stock.

To finish, cook bacon until crisp and remove from pan. Remove all but 3 tablespoons of the drippings. Add onion, pepper and corn, and sauté for 3 minutes. Stir in flour to make a roux. Then cook 3 minutes over medium heat.

Pour in corn stock, stirring constantly. Simmer over low heat for 30 minutes. Add heavy cream and cooked bacon. Season with salt, pepper and thyme. Garnish with wild rice and chicken.

From the chef:

This soup has become a mainstay at The Adolphus. It is, by far, the hotel's most requested recipe.

Tossed Romaine Leaves in a Caesar Cream

2 heads Romaine lettuce,
washed and cut into ½-inch
pieces (drain well)

1 cup Caesar cream
(recipe on following page)

Crushed black pepper

½ cup grated Parmesan

Place one cup of the Caesar cream and the Romaine leaves in a bowl. (A wooden bowl is preferable.) Toss very well to ensure the leaves are coated with the cream. Serve on individual salad plates and garnish with croutons (recipe on following page), Parmesan cheese and black pepper.

From the chef:

Remember that the Romaine leaves should be very dry or the dressing will not coat evenly.

(continued)

Makes 6 servings.

Caesar Cream

2   eggs

2   cups olive oil

½   cup salad oil

½   can anchovies

1   tablespoon red wine vinegar

¼   cup lemon juice

2   cloves garlic

1½   teaspoons salt

1½   teaspoons black pepper

¾   cup Romano cheese

2   teaspoons chopped parsley

¼   cup Dijon-style mustard

1½   teaspoons dry mustard

2   tablespoons Worcestershire
    sauce

Combine anchovies, vinegar, eggs, garlic, parsley, mustards and Worcestershire sauce in a food processor fitted with a metal blade. Blend well. Slowly add the oils until the dressing begins to thicken. (You may want to add a small amount of water to this.) Pour in the rest of the oil. Finish the dressing by adding the remaining ingredients. Chill for at least 2 hours.

From the chef:

If the cream is too thick, thin it with a little water. This is particularly true if the cream is left in the refrigerator overnight.

Baked Croutons

12   slices sourdough bread,
     crusts removed and diced
     (medium)

½   cup olive oil

Heat oven to 325°F. Toss the bread cubes in olive oil and spead them out on a cookie sheet. Bake cubes for 10 minutes or until golden brown.

Makes approximately 3 cups of croutons.

Chicken-Fried Steak with Cream Gravy

6   *three-ounce strip loin steaks, pounded thin*

1½   *cups buttermilk*

2   *cups flour*

1   *teaspoon salt*

1   *tablespoon coarse ground black pepper*

½   *cup olive oil for sautéing*

Dip steaks in buttermilk, coating each completely. As the steaks are removed from the buttermilk, dredge them in flour mixed with salt and pepper. Repeat process (steaks need to be dipped and coated twice). Refrigerate or freeze steaks for 1 to 2 hours before pan-frying.

To fry the steaks, heat the olive oil over a medium heat and completely brown the steaks on both sides. Place steaks in a preheated 350°F oven for 10 minutes to ensure that the steaks are done on the inside.

From the chef:

The breading on the chicken-fried steaks should puff up when fried. It may be necessary to add more olive oil to the skillet as you fry the steaks.

(continued)

Cream Gravy

1 pint heavy cream

2 tablespoons butter

2 tablespoons flour

½ teaspoon coarse ground black
  pepper

  Salt to taste

  Dash Worcestershire sauce

Bring the heavy cream to a boil. (Be careful not to over boil it.) In a separate pan, melt the butter; then add the flour to make a roux. Cook the roux for one minute. Stir in the heavy cream with a wire whip and simmer for 5 minutes. Add the remaining ingredients, stirring constantly.

From the chef:

There really is no secret to making good cream gravy. It's made in a lot of different ways. Try using sausage grease and diced sausage for your biscuits in the morning. Or, you may want to substitute bacon fat for butter to enhance the flavor. Low in cholesterol cream gravy is not!

Mashed Potatoes with Garlic and Horseradish

6 *medium to large potatoes, peeled and quartered*

6 *cloves garlic, crushed*

½ *cup butter*

1 *cup heavy cream*

1 *tablespoon prepared horseradish*

   Salt and pepper to taste

Place potatoes in a large saucepan and cover with water. Bring to a boil. Simmer until potatoes are tender. Drain potatoes in a colander and put them back in the saucepan. Cook at low heat for 2 to 3 minutes to remove any excess water. Add the rest of the ingredients as the potatoes are mashed. (Use any method to mash the potatoes.)

From the chef:

Mashed potatoes are making a comeback in commercial kitchens throughout the country. The lowly potato has become the haute potato, as chefs experiment with new ways of preparing the old standbys. Using garlic and horseradish is just one technique for enhancing the flavor. Experiment with other herbs and spices.

Makes 4 servings.

Harvester Beans with Bacon and Onions

2 quarts water

1 tablespoon salt

5 strips bacon, diced

1 small onion, diced (small)

1 pound harvester beans,
   cleaned

   Salt and pepper to taste

In a medium-size pot, bring the water to a boil. Add one tablespoon of salt. Submerge the beans in the boiling water and cook until the beans are al dente (approximately five minutes). Remove the beans from the water and drain. While the beans are cooking, start frying the bacon. When the bacon is partially cooked, add the diced onions. Stir in the beans and season with salt and pepper.

From the chef:

Some Texans say you can't eat chicken-fried steak without green beans. If you agree, this recipe is excellent.

Multi-Grain Rolls

1¾ cups bread flour

2 tablespoons cornmeal

2 tablespoons oatmeal

1½ tablespoons semolina

¼ cup rye flour

¼ cup cracked wheat

½ cup malt flakes

2½ teaspoons salt

⅓ cup brown sugar

2 tablespoons plus 2½ teaspoons instant yeast

¾ cup water

¼ cup vegetable oil

1 tablespoon honey

2½ teaspoons molasses

Honey Glaze

⅓ cup honey mixed with ½ cup water

Using a dough hook, mix all dry ingredients in a small mixing bowl for 30 seconds. Pour in all liquids and mix for 2 minutes or until the dough pulls cleanly away from the sides of the bowl. (If it does not, add a touch more flour.)

Place dough on a floured work surface. Take a rolling pin to roll out the dough to 1-inch thickness. Cut into desired shapes. Let the dough rise in a warm place until it is 1½ times its original size.

Preheat oven to 350°F.

Place rolls on a floured cookie sheet and bake for 8 to 10 minutes. Brush rolls with Honey Glaze immediately after baking.

From the chef:

Many of these ingredients are found in health food stores. But it's worth the extra effort to find them. This is another Adolphus recipe frequently requested by our guests.

Makes 8 servings.

Ginger Applesauce Cake

2 cups sugar
1 cup soft butter
2 cups applesauce
1 cup pecan pieces
1 cup raisins
3 cups cake flour
1¾ teaspoons baking powder
1 teaspoon cinnamon
1½ teaspoons ground ginger

Cream butter and sugar until light and fluffy. Add applesauce, pecans and raisins. (Raisins should be dredged in ¼ cup flour.) Sift together the rest of the flour and the remaining dry ingredients. Then combine this with the applesauce mixture. Add vanilla, and pour the mixture into a greased cake pan. Bake at 325F° for approximately 1 hour and 20 minutes, or until a toothpick comes clean when inserted in the center of the cake.

AUTUMN

Universally loved, pizza offers chefs a unique way to please almost any palate. The dough can vary; the crusts can be thick or thin; and, the toppings can be traditional or exotic. In our kitchens, we prefer to be daringly different, taking pizza a leap beyond the standard fare. Its an ideal outlet for creativity and experimentation — and the staff really enjoys the "test tastings." Our Adolphus pizzas are especially appealing to business travelers, who enjoy a culinary diversion when they are on the road. Pizza is also often on the menu at the children's parties held during the annual Adolphus/Children's Christmas Parade. But, as you might guess, we keep the toppings fairly simple.

PIZZA

Scampi Pizza with Feta Cheese and
Greek Olives

Vegetarian Pizza

❖

(Selected items pictured on page 123)

Scampi Pizza

1   nine-inch pizza shell
    (recipe on following page)

4   *jumbo shrimp, peeled and deveined*

2   *cloves garlic, crushed*

1   *bunch parsley, chopped*

1   *cup feta cheese*

½   *cup Greek olives, pitted and sliced*

1   *tablespoon olive oil*

½   *cup fresh basil, diced*

½   *cup pizza sauce*
    (recipe on following page)

Sauté the shrimp in a skillet filled with the tablespoon of olive oil. When the shrimp is ¾ done, add the garlic and finish cooking. Remove from the pan and cool.

Lay out the pizza shell on a clean work surface. Cover just to the edges with pizza sauce. (Leave a small amount of edge unsauced for the crust.) Sprinkle the rest of the ingredients evenly over the top of the pizza shell. Bake in a 450°F oven for approximately 6 to 8 minutes. The pie should sit 5 minutes before slicing.

New Year's Eve, p. 181

Pizza Dough

7 cups flour

1½ cups warm water

1 tablespoon salt

2 teaspoons sugar

1 tablespoon olive oil

1½ teaspoons baker's yeast

From the chef:

The thickness of the crust depends on the amount of yeast in the dough and the thickness of the rolled dough prior to prebaking. Try adding ¼ teaspoon of yeast to this recipe and experiment by adding a little more each time. The diameter of the crust corresponds to the weight of the dough ball before rolling. For example, this recipe calls for a 9-ounce dough ball. So, the dough should be rolled out to form a 9" circle.

Measure the flour, sugar and salt into a mixing bowl. Using the dough hook, mix for a few seconds. Dissolve yeast in lukewarm water (100°F). Add the olive oil to the water.

Combine the water and flour mixtures using the dough hook. Mix for 15 minutes. Remove the dough hook and cover bowl with a piece of plastic wrap or a warm moist towel. Place the bowl in a warm place (over the oven or on top of the refrigerator) and let it rise for 2 hours.

Remove the dough from the bowl and separate it into four 9-ounce pieces. Form the pieces of dough into balls. Place the balls on a pan and cover with plastic or warm moist towels. Allow the balls to rise for 1½ hours.

Stretch the dough into a pizza crust by starting in the middle with both hands, rotating the dough and working toward the outer edge. When the dough is about 9" to 10" in diameter, place dough on a pizza stone or a cookie sheet. Prebake shell for 5 minutes at 450°F.

Christmas Tea, p. 167

Makes 2 cups.

Quick Pizza Sauce

2   cups canned pizza sauce
1   teaspoon garlic powder
1   teaspoon dried basil
1   teaspoon dried oregano
1   teaspoon dried marjoram

Mix all ingredients together and refrigerate.

From the chef:

It may come as a surprise that we recommend using a canned pizza sauce. However, if you purchase a good quality pizza sauce and add a few dry ingredients, you will have exactly what your local pizza parlor serves. Who could ask for more?

Vegetarian Pizza

6   cloves garlic, cleaned

10   shallot bulbs, cleaned

1   summer squash, diced
    (medium)

1   zucchini, diced (medium)

8   large mushroom, stems
    removed

6   Roma tomatoes, peeled,
    seeded and diced (medium)

2   teaspoons fresh thyme,
    cleaned and diced

2   tablespoon fresh basil,
    cleaned and diced

2   tablespoons fresh oregano,
    cleaned and diced

¼   cup olive oil

    Salt and pepper

2   cups mozzarella cheese

To peel and seed the tomatoes, place them in a pot of boiling water for a 15-second count. Remove from the boiling water and shock in an ice-water bath to cool quickly. Cut the tomatoes in half and squeeze out the seeds. Dice and set aside.

In a large, heavy-bottomed skillet, warm the olive oil over medium heat. Drop in the garlic and shallots and sauté slowly. Make sure the pan is not too hot. As the garlic and shallots start to brown, add the rest of the ingredients, continuing to sauté slowly. (You can also put the skillet in the oven and let the vegetables stew for one hour. But, the skillet has to be oven safe.) Remove from heat and season. Refrigerate until ready to use.

Place the prebaked pizza crust on a pizza stone and spread on a little pizza sauce. Cover the pizza sauce with the vegetable topping. Add the grated mozzarella cheese and bake in a 450°F oven for approximately 6 to 8 minutes. You should allow the pie to sit for 5 minutes before slicing.

From the chef:

Before putting the tomato in the boiling water, core the tomato and make an "X" on the opposite end from the core . This makes the tomato easier to peel.

Brush a little basil pesto (recipe on following page) on the prebaked pizza crust (recipe on preceding page) before covering with the topping.

Makes 3 cups.

Basil Pesto

2   *cups fresh basil leaves*

1   *cup olive oil*

3   *cloves garlic*

   Salt and pepper to taste

Place the basil leaves and garlic in a food processor fitted with a metal blade. While the machine is running, slowly pour in the olive oil. Finish with salt and pepper.

From the chef:

Pestos have grown in popularity in recent years. Traditionally, pine nuts and warm Parmesan cheese were added to the basic recipe of basil and olive oil. Today, however, pestos are made with all kinds of fresh herbs, nuts and flavored oils.

WINTER

AT THE ADOLPHUS

WINTER

With the rich scents of evergreen
boughs, cinnamon, and bayberry filling
the air, friends gather for a cozy
afternoon tea beside the towering
Christmas tree in the hotel's lobby
living room. Tea time is a popular
Adolphus tradition kept throughout the
year, but it becomes especially
appealing — almost magical — during
the holiday season.

CHRISTMAS TEA

Fresh Strawberries with Devonshire Cream

Assorted Finger Sandwiches

Curried Chicken with Raisins and Apples
Sliced Cucumber with Boursin Cream Cheese
Smoked Salmon with Alfalfa Sprouts

Assorted Sweets

Miniature Eclairs
Almond Macaroons
Almond Meringue Macaroons
Washington Squares
Shortbread
Scones

❖

(selected items pictured on page 160)

Makes 6 servings.

Fresh Strawberries with Devonshire Cream

18   large flawless strawberries

1½   cups Devonshire cream

From the chef:

When selecting the strawberries for afternoon tea, look for ones that don't have any blemishes. Soak the berries in ice water for 20 minutes. Pat them dry on a paper towel.

Devonshire cream can be found in specialty food stores. Some people know it as clotted cream. Both are acceptable. When neither are available, slightly whipped heavy cream may also be served with the strawberries.

Finger Sandwiches

Curried Chicken with Raisins and Apples

3 slices wheat bread

4 beefsteak tomato slices
   (very thin)

1 8-ounce boneless chicken
   breast

2 green onions, diced

½ apple, peeled, cored, and
   diced (small)

¼ cup raisins

1 rib celery, diced (small)

¼ cup mayonnaise

1 teaspoon curry powder

1 tablespoon olive oil

   Salt to taste

Heat the olive oil in a frying pan and sauté the chicken breast over medium to high heat until completely cooked (approximately 10 minutes). After letting the chicken breast cool, dice the chicken into ½-inch cubes and place in a mixing bowl. Combine with the diced onions, apple, raisins, celery, mayonnaise, curry powder and olive oil. Season with salt to taste.

Place a tomato slice on the first slice of bread, followed by half of the chicken salad and another tomato slice. Place the second slice of bread on top and repeat the filling layers, finishing with the third slice of bread. Trim crusts and cut sandwich into quarters.

Finger Sandwiches

Cucumber with Boursin Cream Cheese and Smoked Salmon with Alfalfa Sprouts

3 slices white bread

3 slices pumpernickel

8 ounces cream cheese

2 ounces Boursin

1 bunch watercress,
washed and stemmed

6 cucumber slices,
⅛-inch thick

3 ounces smoked salmon

½ ounce alfalfa sprouts

Place the cream cheese and Boursin in a food processor. Blend until smooth and soft. Remove from processor and reserve 6 ounces of the mixture for the salmon mousse.

Spread the blended cream cheese on 1 piece of white bread and place cucumber slices on top. Spread cream cheese on second slice of white bread and place on top of the cucumbers, cheese side down. Spread cheese on top side of the second slice of bread and put watercress leaves on the cheese. Spread the rest of the cheese mix on the third slice of bread and place it cheese side down on top of watercress. Cut the crusts off of the bread and slice into four finger sandwiches.

For the smoked salmon mousse, place the smoked salmon in a food processor and mince. Add the remaining 6 ounces of cream cheese mixture and mix until incorporated.

Spread mousse on 1 slice of pumpernickel. Place half of the alfalfa sprouts on top of mousse. Spread mousse on the second slice of pumpernickel and place on top of the alfalfa sprouts. Spread more mousse on the top side of the second slice of bread and place the remaining alfalfa sprouts on top of the mousse. Finally, spread the mousse on the third slice of pumpernickel. Place it mousse side down on top of alfalfa sprouts. Trim off crusts and cut into quarters. (Some mousse may be left over, depending upon how thickly it is spread.)

Miniature Eclairs

1½ cups water
1½ sticks unsalted butter
¼ teaspoon salt
2¼ cups all-purpose flour
9 eggs

Bring water and butter to a boil in a saucepan. Add flour and salt all at once. Stir with a wooden spoon until the mixture forms a ball in the center of the pan. Remove from heat and immediately add eggs, one at a time. Beat with the spoon to form a smooth paste after each addition.

Put paste in a pastry bag fitted with a plain or star tip. Pipe the paste onto a greased baking sheet, forming 3 dozen miniature eclairs (long and narrow ovals). Bake at 400°F for approximately 15 minutes. Reduce heat to 325°F and bake for another 10 minutes. Remove from the oven and cool.

When eclairs are cool, they can be sliced and filled with pastry cream (recipe on page 32) or whipped cream. Top with chocolate and powdered sugar.

From the chef:

Experiment with different fillings and toppings. Fruits and nuts add an interesting flavor.

Almond Macaroons

1¾ cups almond paste

½ cup granulated sugar

½ cup egg whites

1 teaspoon vanilla ·

2 drops egg-shade food
   coloring (optional)

Beat almond paste and sugar in a small mixing bowl. Add egg whites very slowly so no lumps form. Pour in vanilla and optional egg-shade food coloring. Spoon onto greased baking sheet. Bake at 350°F for 10 to 15 minutes until golden brown.

From the chef:

If this mixture is overbeaten, the macaroons will bake with cracks or cavities in the center. Mix just until all ingredients are incorporated.

The macaroons may be dipped in melted chocolate when cooled.

Almond paste is available in the specialty sections of most supermarkets.

Almond Meringue Macaroons

1½ cups almond powder
2½ cups sifted powdered sugar
  5 egg whites
 ⅓ cup granulated sugar

Blend almond powder and powdered sugar in a small mixing bowl. In a separate mixing bowl, whip the egg whites and granulated sugar until firm peaks are formed. Gently fold dry ingredients into egg whites. Drop by teaspoon onto a paper-lined baking sheet. Bake 10 to 15 minutes at 375°F until light brown. Do not try to remove from paper until completely cooled.

Sandwich two macaroons together with raspberry or apricot jam. Dust with powdered sugar.

From the chef:

Almond powder can be found in most specialty food shops.

Washington Squares

2 sticks unsalted butter, melted

2 cups graham cracker crumbs

1⅓ cups chocolate chips

2¼ cups shredded coconut

3½ cups pecan pieces

2½ cans (14 ounces each) condensed milk

Pour melted butter onto a baking sheet and spread evenly. In this order, sprinkle graham cracker crumbs, chocolate chips, coconut and pecans evenly over the butter. Using a second baking sheet of the same size, press down on the mixture to compress it tightly. Pour the condensed milk over the top of the compressed mixture. Bake at 360°F for 15 to 20 minutes or until golden brown. Cool and cut into squares.

From the chef:

You will need a baking sheet with 1-inch sides to do this recipe as written.

Amaretto Shortbread

3 sticks unsalted butter

1⅓ cups sugar

2 egg yolks (reserve whites)

2 tablespoons Amaretto

2 teaspoons orange zest

2 cups cake flour

1¾ cups bread flour

Sliced almonds

Granulated sugar

Cream butter and sugar until light and fluffy. Add egg yolks, Amaretto, and orange zest. Mix in flour until well incorporated. Spread mixture evenly onto a greased baking sheet. Brush top with egg whites. Sprinkle with sliced almonds and sugar. Bake at 325°F for 20 to 30 minutes or until golden brown. Shortbread is done when a toothpick inserted in the middle comes out clean. Cool slightly and cut into pieces (size depends on personal taste).

From the chef:

Shortbread should be cut while still warm. It becomes too brittle if it cools completely.

Scones

2	cups bread flour
2	cups cake flour
2½	tablespoons baking powder
1	teaspoon salt
1	tablespoon sugar
1	cup vegetable shortening
1	cup milk
1	cup sour cream
2	cups raisins
1	beaten egg to brush top of scones

Place dry ingredients in mixing bowl with shortening and blend with fingers. Mix milk and sour cream together and add to dry ingredients. Do not over mix. Sprinkle in the raisins.

Using your hands, pat dough out on a floured work surface. Dough should be ¾- to 1-inch thick. Cut with small biscuit cutter and place on a paper-lined baking sheet. Brush with egg mixture. Bake at 375°F for 15 to 20 minutes or until golden brown. Serve immediately.

From the chef:

Scones are traditionally served with jams and clotted cream. Whipped cream can be substituted. When Her Majesty Queen Elizabeth II had afternoon tea at The Adolphus, she used only fresh butter on her scones.

Valentine's Day, p. 199 and
Cocktail Hour, p. 209

WINTER

On New Year's Eve, a table for two in The French Room is one of the most sought-after reservations in the city. Sophisticated, yet warm and inviting, this gourmet dining room fills twice during the evening. Guests in black-tie come and go, with dancing just outside in the hotel's lobby living room. Often at midnight, rare vintages from its wine cellar are uncorked to ensure that the toasts have a noble accompaniment. The hotel's original owner, beer baron Adolphus Busch, considered The French Room one of his crown jewels, and on New Year's Eve every facet sparkles.

New Year's Eve in the French Room

Steamed Mussels

Black and White Fettuccine Alfredo

Black Bean Soup with
Sour Cream Pico de Gallo

Flourless Chocolate Cake with
White Chocolate Mousse

❖

(selected items pictured on page 159)

Makes 2 servings.

Steamed Mussels

24 mussels, scrubbed and debearded

1 teaspoon garlic

1 teaspoon shallots

1 tablespoon fresh thyme

¼ cup white wine

½ cup heavy cream

1 tablespoon olive oil

Heat the olive oil over medium heat and sauté the garlic, shallots and fresh thyme for one minute. Pour in the white wine and heavy cream. Bring to a boil. Add mussels and cover the skillet. Simmer mussels until the shells completely open. Remove the mussels from the skillet and reduce cream by ½.

Serve the mussels in a large bowl with the sauce on the side.

From the chef:

Before cleaning the mussels, let them soak in the sink for ½ hour. Use a scrub pad to help remove the beards.

Black and White Fettuccine Alfredo

¼ pound egg fettuccine

¼ pound squid-ink fettuccine

1 teaspoon garlic, crushed

1½ cups heavy cream

½ cup Parmesan cheese

Black pepper from grinder

2 tablespoons olive oil

Salt to taste

Fresh basil (optional)

Fresh parsley (optional)

Bring a large pot of water to a boil and add a pinch of salt. Boil the pasta until it is tender but still firm to the bite. Remove from the boiling water and cool down in cold water. Rinse and drain in a colander.

In a saucepan, heat the olive oil and sauté the garlic for 10 seconds. Pour in the heavy cream. Bring to a simmer and add the Parmesan cheese. Reduce the cream and cheese until it reaches the desired thickness. Stir in the pasta. Season with the black pepper and herbs (optional).

From the chef:

Squid-ink pasta can be found in specialty grocery stores. Squid ink is used to color the pasta black. There is absolutely no flavor imparted by the squid ink.

Makes 2½ quarts.

Black Bean Soup

5   slices bacon, diced

1   small onion, diced (small)

3   cloves garlic, minced

3   cups black beans, rinsed

3   quarts chicken stock or water

  Salt and pepper to taste

In a medium, heavy-gauged sauce pot, cook bacon over medium heat for 5 minutes. Add the onions and continue to cook until the onions are translucent. Sprinkle in the garlic and cook one more minute. Add the black beans and pour in the chicken stock. Bring the soup to a boil, then reduce the heat to a simmer. Let the soup simmer for 1½ to 2 hours.

Blend the mixture in a blender until it is smooth. Season with salt and pepper to taste. Serve hot. Garnish with pico de gallo and a dollop of sour cream.

From the chef:

The soup may need to be thinned, depending on individual taste. Add either a little chicken stock or water.

Flourless Chocolate Cake

14 egg yolks
1½ cups sugar
10 egg whites
1 cup sugar
1½ cups cocoa

Beat egg yolks and 1¾ cups sugar in a stainless steel mixing bowl until light and fluffy. The mixture will be a pale yellow.

In a second stainless steel bowl, beat egg whites and 1 cup sugar until it forms stiff peaks. Gently fold sifted cocoa powder into egg yolk mixture. Pour in the egg white mixture, folding gently, until both mixtures are incorporated.

Pour batter into a 10-inch greased springform cake pan. Bake at 360°F for about 45 minutes.

Let the cake cool in the pan. Cake will sink considerably, but this is normal. Once cake has cooled, top with white chocolate mousse (recipe on following page). Make the mousse level with the top of the pan. Refrigerate 3 to 4 hours. Remove from pan and serve.

From the chef:

Rubbing a warm, damp rag around outside of the pan will help release cake from the sides.

White Chocolate Mousse

10 *ounces white chocolate*

5 *egg whites*

⅓ *cup sugar*

2 *cups heavy cream*

3 *sheets gelatin*

¼ *cup Grand Marnier*

Melt white chocolate in a double boiler. Set aside when the chocolate is completely melted. Whip cream until stiff and set aside. Whip egg whites with sugar until stiff; leave them in the bowl. After gelatin has bloomed and is strained of excess water, melt along with Grand Marnier.

In this order, fold the following ingredients into the egg whites: white chocolate, whipped cream and gelatin. Fold until completely incorporated.

WINTER

With the end of the holidays comes a taste for the basics: meat and potatoes menus that warm the body and rekindle the spirit. At The Adolphus, we keep plenty of roast pork, beef, and chicken on hand and enhance them with fresh seasonal trimmings. The temperature in Dallas sometimes drops below zero. A thin veneer of ice and snow has been known to shut down schools and businesses, close airports, and keep guests and staff alike inside our cozy confines a little longer than planned.

ICED IN

Oven-baked Onion Soup with Three Cheeses

Roast Loin of Pork with Red Bliss Potatoes,
Seasonal Vegetables and Red Onion Marmalade
with Pork Gravy

Sauerkraut with Apple-smoked Bacon

Fresh Applesauce

Warm Herb Bread

Chunky Peanut Butter Pie on a Kahlua Cream

❖

(Roast Loin of Pork pictured on page 142)

Makes 4 servings.

Oven-baked Onion Soup

8	onions, thinly sliced
½	cup olive oil
1½	ounces Dry Sack sherry
1½	ounces Cognac
1½	ounces white wine
2	quarts chicken stock
2	tablespoons fresh thyme
	Salt and pepper to taste

Using a large soup pot, heat the olive oil over a medium high heat and add the sliced onions. Sauté the onions until they turn golden brown. Pour in the sherry, Cognac, and wine. Reduce to almost dry. Add the rest of the ingredients and simmer for 30 minutes. Remove from heat and cool.

You will need oven-proof soup bowls to finish the soup.

To Finish Soup:

4	slices Swiss cheese
4	slices mozzarella
4	slices provolone
3	cups onion soup
4	croutons per bowl, ½-inch cubes

Fill the soup crocks with onion soup and place the croutons on top. Lay one slice of each of the three cheeses on the croutons. Place in a 350°F oven and bake until the cheese is browned.

From the chef:

Croutons can be made from regular white bread or whatever is desirable.

Roast Loin of Pork

1 center cut pork loin
1 tablespoon garlic
1 teaspoon coarse ground pepper
½ cup fresh sage
½ cup fresh rosemary
½ cup fresh thyme
2 tablespoons olive oil
Salt to taste

Heat oven to 350°F. Mix the seasonings with the olive oil and rub into the pork loin. Place the loin in a roasting pan and roast for approximately 90 minutes.

Red Bliss Potatoes and Seasonal Vegetables

8 red bliss potatoes (one per person), cut in half
2 pieces carrot
2 pieces turnip
2 pieces onion

Prepare the potatoes and other vegetables. Roast with the pork loin.

From the chef:

The roasting time depends on your oven. Pork loin should be cooked thoroughly.

Makes 8 to 10 servings.

Red Onion Marmalade

4 medium red onions, thinly sliced

2 tablespoons oil

½ teaspoon butter

2 tablespoons grenadine

½ teaspoon balsamic vinegar

1 teaspoon sugar

Pinch of fresh thyme

Heat olive oil and butter in a large skillet over medium heat. Add the onions and sauté them until they are golden brown. Stir occasionally so the onions do not burn. When the onions are done, add the remaining ingredients and sauté for one more minute. Cover the skillet and turn off the burner. After 2 to 3 minutes, remove the onion marmalade from the skillet and serve immediately.

From the chef:

Browning the onions takes a relatively long time. It must be done slowly over a medium flame. Remember, too, that the onions, owing to their high sugar content, will begin to caramelize as they cook. Be patient!

Pork Gravy

From the chef:

When the pork loin is finished, remove it and the vegetables from the roasting pan. Pour some chicken stock or water into the pan. Scrape the bottom of the pan with a spoon and let the liquid simmer until it has reached the desired consistency.

Sauerkraut with Apple-smoked Bacon

2   cups sauerkraut

8   slices bacon

1   large onion, diced (small)

1½   tablespoons red wine vinegar

1   tablespoon brown sugar

Dice the bacon into small pieces and cook until almost done. Add the diced onions and sauté until the onions begin to brown. Remove the bacon grease from the pan and add the rest of the ingredients. Simmer for 20 to 30 minutes.

From the chef:

Fresh or canned sauerkraut should be rinsed before sautéing. This will enhance the flavor and eliminate the taste of brine.

Fresh Applesauce

12–14   apples
   ¾   cup brown sugar
   ¼   cup butter
   ½   cup water
        Juice of one whole lemon
  1½   teaspoon cinnamon

Peel, core, and dice the apples. Place in a large sauce pot with the remaining ingredients and bring to a simmer. As the apples begin to soften, mash them with the back of a spoon or whip. When the apples are sufficiently soft, remove from the pot and chill in the refrigerator.

From the chef:

The choice of apples is up to you. You may also choose to leave the applesauce a little chunky. Adding raisins and nuts to the cooled applesauce is a nice change.

Warm Herb Bread

 2 *cups whole wheat flour*

2½ *cups bread flour*

 2 *tablespoons salt*

 ⅓ *cup instant yeast*

 1 *large onion, diced and sautéed*

 2 *cups Parmesan cheese*

 ½ *teaspoon thyme*

 ¾ *teaspoon pepper*

 1 *teaspoon celery salt*

 1 *teaspoon poultry seasoning*

 ½ *teaspoon parsley flakes*

 ½ *teaspoon dill*

 1 *cup melted butter*

1½ *cups milk*

Place all of the dry ingredients in a mixing bowl. Mix with a dough hook on low speed for approximately 30 seconds. Add the sautéed onions, butter and milk. Mix for 2 minutes. The dough should pull cleanly away from the sides of the mixing bowl. If not, lightly sprinkle in more bread flour until it does.

Remove dough from the bowl and place on a floured work surface. Roll the dough with a floured rolling pin to a ¼-inch thickness. Cut into 2-inch triangles and place on a cookie sheet. After covering with plastic, put it in a warm place. Proof for one hour or until dough doubles in size.

Bake at 350°F for 8 to 10 minutes.

Makes one 10-inch pie.

Chunky Peanut Butter Pie

1	cup cream cheese
½	cup sugar
¾	cup chunky peanut butter
¼	cup milk
1½	cups white chocolate, roughly chopped
5	egg whites
1	cup cream, whipped
3	leaves gelatin

Using a mixer with a paddle, cream the cream cheese, sugar, peanut butter and milk in a small mixing bowl.

Melt chocolate in a double boiler and set aside. Whip the egg whites until stiff and set those aside. After blooming the gelatin, melt over a double boiler.

In this order, fold these ingredients into cream cheese mixture: egg whites, whipped cream and gelatin. Fill the oatmeal fudge pie crust (recipe on following page) with this mixture and refrigerate. Serve each slice on a thin veneer of Kahlua cream sauce (recipe on following page).

Oatmeal Fudge Pie Crust

¾ cup sugar

2½ ounces butter

¼ cup cocoa powder

⅓ cup milk

2 cups oatmeal

¼ cup peanut butter

Boil sugar, butter, cocoa powder and milk for 1 minute. Remove from heat and stir in oatmeal and peanut butter. Pour mixture into a 10-inch pie pan and mold. Let crust harden before pouring in the filling.

Kahlua Cream Sauce

1 pint milk

5 tablespoons sugar

4 egg yolks

1 teaspoon vanilla

   Kahlua to taste

Bring milk to a boil. In a mixing bowl, beat egg yolks with sugar. Combine egg yolk mixture and the hot milk by first adding a small amount of milk to the egg mixture and, then, pouring the warmed egg mixture into the saucepan of hot milk. Heat over medium heat until it is just thick enough to coat the back of a spoon. Remove from stove and pour into a cool bowl. Stir in vanilla and Kahlua to taste.

WINTER

With its rich interiors and European accents, The Adolphus is considered by many to be one of the most romantic hotels in America. Valentine's Day finds the hotel filled with couples taking advantage of the popular "Return to Romance" package. The hotel's French Room is often the setting for marriage proposals where the staff has become accustomed to hiding engagement rings in everything from a sorbet to a raspberry crème brûlée. With nearly a century of gracious hospitality behind it, the hotel greets at least one anniversary couple almost every week. One pair recently checked in for their 71st anniversary!

Valentine's Day

Fresh Oysters in the Shell
with Mignonette Sauce

Cracker Breaded Oysters

Tempura Oysters

Oyster Shooters served with
Chili Cocktail Sauce

Oven~Poached Sole Fillet
filled with Lobster Mousse on a
Cognac Cream Sauce with a Caviar Garnish

Roasted Veal Chop with Tricolored Pearl Onions

Raspberry Crème Brûlée
Jean Banchet

❖

(selected items pictured on page 177)

Fresh Oysters in the Shell

16 oysters

1 lemon, cut into eighths

4 tablespoons champagne vinegar

1 tablespoon chives, finely diced

1 large shallot, finely diced

Sea salt, fine grind

Pepper, fresh ground

Place the oysters in the sink and cover with water. Let oysters soak for 20 minutes, refreshing the water two or three times. Remove oysters from the water, one at a time, and wrap in a towel. Using an oyster knife, open each oyster from the back. Hold the towel securely so that it does not move while the oysters are cut open.

Combine the vinegar, chives and shallots in a stainless steel bowl. Marinate for one hour.

When ready to serve, squeeze lemon wedges over each oyster, reserving four wedges for garnish. Season each oyster with salt and black pepper. Using a teaspoon, pour a small amount of the vinegar mixture on each oyster and serve. Garnish the plates with the remaining lemon wedges.

From the chef:

Opening oysters takes great precaution and care. Practice helps, but use an expert if one is available.

Oysters in the shell are usually served on cracked ice or rock salt. Fresh herbs, mignonette sauce, and lemon wedges work well as garnishes.

The Adolphus serves most of its oyster dishes in February. Oysters arrive daily from both coasts and find their way onto most of our menus.

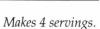
Cracker Breaded Oysters

12 oysters removed from the shell

18 saltine crackers, crushed in a food processor

3 eggs, whipped

1½ cups all-purpose flour

Black pepper from the grinder

1 cup salad or peanut oil

After removing the oysters from the shell, season with a little black pepper and dredge through the flour. Shake off any excess flour. Drop the oysters into beaten eggs, coating thoroughly.

Using a fork, dredge coated oysters in cracker crumbs. (You may want to coat with egg and crackers again to ensure that each is completely covered.) Refrigerate for one hour.

Heat salad or peanut oil in a large heavy skillet over medium heat until it reaches 325°F or begins to bubble when an oyster is placed in the pan. Brown both sides evenly and remove to a cookie sheet. Keep warm in a 325°F oven for up to 5 minutes.

Serve with cocktail sauce and lemon wedges.

From the chef:

Fried oysters are usually served in a basket, but these oysters also make a great garnish for grilled meats, such as filet mignon or sirloin steaks.

Makes 4 servings.

Tempura Oysters

12 oysters removed from the
    shell
1   cup all-purpose flour
¼   cup corn starch
¾   cup water
1   egg
1   teaspoon salad oil
½   teaspoon baking powder
    Salt and pepper to taste
1   cup salad or peanut oil

Place the flour and corn starch in a stainless steel bowl. Pour in water, a little at a time, working the water in with your fingers. Use enough water to form a smooth paste. Add the egg, 1 teaspoon of salad oil, baking powder and salt and pepper. Whip mixture, carefully folding in all ingredients.

Mix the oysters into the tempura batter. Remove with a fork directly into a skillet filled with the hot oil. Fry the oysters until they are a golden brown. Carefully place each oyster on a paper towel and serve immediately.

Serve the tempura oysters with a cocktail sauce or mignonette sauce.

From the chef:

It is important to remove all the lumps from the batter. This is why you should use your fingers. Also, do not work the tempura too much after adding the baking powder. This will break down the activation, and the oysters will not be light enough.

Oyster Shooters

8 oysters, removed from the shell

1 tablespoon prepared horseradish

½ lemon, seeds removed

2 tablespoons cocktail sauce

Tabasco to taste

8 shot glasses

In the bottom of each shot glass, splash a small amount of Tabasco and a small amount of the horseradish. Place one oyster in each shot glass and squeeze a bit of lemon juice on each one. Top off each oyster with cocktail sauce and serve.

From the chef:

With the addition of a small amount of vodka or tequila, each shooter becomes a little more interesting.

Chili Cocktail Sauce

1 bottle of ketchup

1 bottle of chili sauce

½ tablespoon prepared horseradish

½ lemon, seeds removed

Splash Worcestershire sauce

Splash Tabasco

Combine all the ingredients in a stainless steel mixing bowl. Marinate for one hour in the refrigerator before serving.

From the chef:

The amount of each ingredient in this recipe is based on personal taste. You may also want to add 2 tablespoons of sour cream and 1 shot of Cognac to give it some extra zip.

Makes 2 servings.

Oven-Poached Sole Fillet

6 *two-ounce sole fillets*

1 *cup lobster mousse*

½ *cup dry vermouth*

2 *tablespoons olive oil*

¾ *cup Cognac cream sauce*

1 *ounce black caviar*

Lobster Mousse

1 *1¼-pound lobster, cleaned, shells reserved*

4 *jumbo shrimp, cleaned, shells reserved*

½ *cup heavy cream*

1 *egg*

1 *teaspoon lobster base*

  White pepper

Remove the lobster meat from the shells and save the shells for the sauce. In a food processor, combine the lobster meat with the shrimp, eggs, lobster base and white pepper. Grind to a fine puree. Remove the bowl from the machine and put it in the freezer for about 30 minutes. Allow the bowl and its contents to get very cold. Place the bowl back on the machine and blend in the cream. Remove the mousse from the mixing bowl and keep very cold in the refrigerator.

Place 2 sole fillets on an oiled baking sheet pan. Top each fillet with half the mousse. Cover these fillets with the four remaining fillets (two per fillet; tented like an inverted "V"). Pour the vermouth over each fillet. Season with salt and pepper.

Fillets can be prepared to this point and then refrigerated for up to 2 hours. When you are about ready to serve, place the fillets in a preheated 350°F oven for approximately 10 to 12 minutes. Remove from the oven and serve immediately with the Cognac sauce (recipe on following page) under the fish. Spoon the caviar over the top of the fillets.

Cognac Cream Sauce

Lobster shells

Shrimp shells

1 carrot, small dice

½ onion, small dice

1 rib celery, small dice

1 clove garlic, crushed

2 shots Cognac

1 shot dry vermouth

1 shot sherry wine

½ teaspoon lobster base

1½ cups heavy cream

1 teaspoon tomato paste

1 tablespoon olive oil

1 teaspoon fresh tarragon, finely diced

Salt and white pepper

Heat the olive oil in a large heavy skillet. Add lobster and shrimp shells and brown them. Put in the celery, onions, carrots and garlic. Begin to brown the vegetables. Remove the skillet from the stove and pour in the Cognac, vermouth and sherry wine. Carefully place the skillet back on the stove. If using a gas flame, a small flame will appear in the pan. This is the alcohol burning away from the liquor. When the flame begins to evaporate, add the lobster base, cream tomato paste and tarragon. Reduce by half. Strain through a sieve. Season with salt and white pepper. Reserve and keep warm.

From the chef:

This recipe may seem difficult and a bit long. But, remember, you are doing this for your Valentine. Who could be more deserving?

Since the price of lobster tends to drop during the summer months, you may want to indulge your sweetheart then, too.

Roasted Veal Chop

2   bone-in center-cut veal
    chops, preferably with
    tenderloin

1   cup tricolored pearl onions,
    cleaned

1   cup cooked spinach

1   tablespoon maitre d' butter
    Salt
    Pepper from the grinder

1   tablespoon olive oil

Rub a little of the olive oil on both chops and season both sides with salt and pepper. Marinate for 20 to 30 minutes at room temperature. Place the rest of the olive oil in a large ovenproof skillet and heat over a medium flame until it is very hot. Brown the chops on both sides. Remove the chops from the pan. Place pearl onions in the skillet and reduce to medium-low heat. After cooking the onions, put the chops back into the pan for 5 minutes. Place the pan in a 375°F oven and roast chops for 10 to 12 minutes. Just before removing from the oven, add the spinach and half of the maitre d' butter. Cook for an additional 2 to 3 minutes.

Remove skillet from the oven and place the meat on a serving platter. Pour the onions and spinach over the meat, and spoon remaining butter over the meat and serve.

Maitre d' Butter

½   cup butter

1¼ teaspoons garlic powder
    Dash of Worcestershire
    sauce
    Dash of Tabasco

¼   teaspoon chives

¼   teaspoon parsley

½   teaspoon cracked pepper

Combine all ingredients in a small mixing bowl and blend thoroughly. This butter freezes well and can be served with many different dishes.

From the chef:

These veal chops are especially delicious when grilled. Also, if the pearl onions are too large, you may have to blanch them in boiling water for 1 to 2 minutes to ensure that they soften in the cooking process.

Raspberry Crème Brûlée Jean Banchet

15	egg yolks
1	cup sugar
2	cups heavy cream
2	cups half-and-half
3	oranges, juice and zest
¼	cup Grand Marnier
2	pints raspberries

Heat oven to 250°F.

In a mixing bowl, combine yolks, sugar and Grand Marnier. Whip vigorously until mixture turns pale yellow. Add the zest and the orange juice. Set aside.

In a large pot over high heat, bring to a boil the heavy cream and the half-and-half. Pour the hot cream slowly into the egg mixture while whipping continuously. Remove the foam. Pour this mixture into ovenproof containers whose bottoms are lined with the fresh raspberries. Cook in a water bath in the oven for 1½ hours. Refrigerate for about 2 to 3 hours before serving.

From the chef:

Before serving, sprinkle the tops with granulated sugar. Put the containers under the broiler to caramelize the sugar. The sugar should crack when a spoon touches it.

WINTER

When the hotel's Louis XIV clock strikes five o'clock, guests begin to gather in the cozy alcoves that surround the antique Steinway in the lobby living room. The pianist plays jazz. The talk is of acquisitions and mergers, stock options, and millions lost and won. Rich hors d'oeuvres — like so many Fabergé jewels — are passed on silver trays, while orders are taken for Manhattans, Gibsons, Champagne Cocktails, and Margaritas, the unofficial drink of the Southwest. It's elegant; it's sophisticated. It's the cocktail hour at The Adolphus.

THE COCKTAIL HOUR

Sweet Manhattan

Spicy Bloody Mary

Martini

Margarita

Champagne Cocktail

Smoked Salmon Mousse with Caviar on
Toast Rounds

Garlic Shrimp on Cucumber Rounds

Deep-Fried Crab Fritters

❖

(selected items pictured on page 178)

Makes one drink.

Sweet Manhattan

1½ ounces bourbon or rye
½ ounce sweet Italian vermouth
   Dash of Angostura bitters
   Maraschino cherry

Pour the bourbon and vermouth over cracked ice in a cocktail shaker. Add the bitters and stir with a long bar spoon. Strain into a stemmed cocktail glass. Garnish with the cherry.

From the chef:

For a dry Manhattan, substitute dry vermouth for the sweet vermouth. For a Rob Roy, substitute Scotch for the bourbon or rye.

The perfect Manhattan is made with 1½ ounces bourbon and ¼ ounce each of sweet and dry vermouth.

Garnish with a lemon twist.

Spicy Bloody Mary

1½   ounces vodka

6   ounces Bloody Mary mix

1   celery rib with leaves

1   wedge of lime

1   tall glass of ice

Pour the vodka over the ice. Add the mix. Garnish the glass with the celery and lime.

THE MIX:

1   cup V-8 vegetable juice

½   teaspoon horseradish

    Dash of Tabasco sauce

½   teaspoon Worcestershire sauce

    Dash of celery salt

    Dash of black pepper

½   lemon, juiced

Mix together the V-8, horseradish, Tabasco, Worcestershire, celery salt, black pepper and lemon juice. Chill well.

Martini

1½   *ounces gin*
½   *ounce dry vermouth*
  Martini olive or twist of lemon zest

Pour the gin and vermouth over cracked ice in a cocktail shaker. Shake well. Strain into a very cold, stemmed cocktail glass. Garnish with an olive or a lemon twist.

From the chef:

For an extra dry martini increase the gin and add just a touch of vermouth. If you prefer vodka martinis, use vodka instead of gin. Add a pickled onion, and you have a Gibson.

Margarita

9 ounces tequila

3 ounces triple sec

1 six-ounce can frozen lime
concentrate

Coarse salt

Lime wedge

In a blender filled with ice, blend tequila, triple sec and lime juice.

Rub the rim of a tall glass with a lime wedge. Dip the rim of the glass in coarse salt. Pour the blended mixture into the glass and garnish with a lime wedge.

Makes one drink.

Champagne Cocktail

1	sugar cube
	Dash of orange bitters
½	*ounce Cognac*
6	*ounces champagne*
1	*twist of orange or lemon zest*

Place the sugar cube in the champagne glass. Add the dash of bitters. Pour in Cognac and champagne. Garnish with the orange or lemon zest.

Smoked Salmon Mousse with Caviar

4   slices white bread

½   pound smoked salmon

¼   pound cream cheese

    Dash of Tabasco

    Dash of Worcestershire
    sauce

½   teaspoon butter

1   ounce black caviar

In a food processor fitted with a metal blade, combine the smoked salmon and cream cheese. Mix on high speed until these ingredients are smooth. Add the Tabasco and Worcestershire sauce and mix well. Remove the mixture from the bowl and put in a pastry bag fitted with a star tip.

Trim the crust from the bread. Using a small round cutter, cut out bread rounds and place them on a baking sheet. Brush each piece of bread with butter and brown in a preheated 350°F oven.

Pipe the salmon mousse onto the toast rounds. Garnish with caviar.

Makes 8 servings.

Garlic Shrimp on Cucumber Rounds

1 large cucumber

8 jumbo shrimp

3 cloves garlic, crushed

¼ cup chopped parsley

2 tablespoons olive oil

1 tablespoon butter

Salt and coarse ground black pepper to taste

Strip the cucumber down the outside with a peeler, leaving a little of the green skin intact. Lay the cucumber down on its side and cut into even slices, ¾ inch thick. Place the cucumber slices on a clean work surface and season with salt. Set aside in the refrigerator.

Clean and peel the shrimp completely. Combine with the garlic, parsley and olive oil in a small stainless steel bowl. Marinate for 1 to 2 hours. Heat a skillet over medium heat and sauté the shrimp slowly until they are fully cooked. Remove from the pan and cool.

Slice each shrimp in half, lengthwise, reserving one piece for each cucumber. Using a sharp knife or a food processor, dice the remaining shrimp into very small pieces. Mix the shrimp with the butter, forming a paste. Reserve.

To assemble, pat dry each cucumber slice with a paper towel. Spread a small amount of the shrimp paste on top of each cucumber. Garnish with the reserved shrimp pieces. Serve immediately.

Deep-Fried Crab Fritters

1   cup choux paste (see eclair recipe on page 171)

1   pound lump crab meat

1   yellow pepper, diced (very small)

1   red pepper, diced (very small)

1   small red onion, diced (very small)

2   tablespoons chives, finely diced

    Salt and pepper to taste

1   tablespoon olive oil

1½ cups olive oil for frying

In a sauté pan, heat the one tablespoon olive oil and sauté the peppers and onions. When the onions become transparent, remove and cool. Combine the choux paste, crab meat, peppers, onions and chives in a medium-size mixing bowl. Season with salt and pepper. Form the mix into little patties and refrigerate for one hour.

Heat the 1½ cups of olive oil in a large heavy skillet and fry the fritters until golden brown. Remove from the pan and pat dry on a paper towel. Serve immediately.

Index